RUGBY LEAGUE
in the 'Seventies

RUGBY LEAGUE JOURNAL
PUBLISHING

Volume Four in the 'Rugby League Journal History Series'

Pictured:
The first issue of 'Open Rugby'
published in May, 1976.

This book is dedicated to the original spirit of 'Open Rugby' - 1976 to 1998.

First published in Great Britain in 2013 by
Rugby League Journal Publishing
P.O.Box 22, Egremont, Cumbria, CA23 3WA

ISBN 978-09548355-8-3

Written, edited and designed by Harry Edgar
Marketing and promotion by Ruth Edgar
Printed by The Firpress Group Limited

Front cover pictures:
Frank Myler proudly holds the Ashes trophy for Great Britain in 1970;
George Fairbairn kicks for Great Britain in the 1978 Ashes Test series;
Alex Murphy lifts the Challenge Cup for Leigh at Wembley on 1971.
Frontispiece picture:
Mike Nicholas jumps for joy as Warrington win the 1974 Challenge Cup Final.

RUGBY LEAGUE JOURNAL
PUBLISHING

P.O. Box 22, Egremont, Cumbria, CA23 3WA
E-Mail: rugbyleague.journal@sky.com   Telephone: 01946 811005
www.rugbyleaguejournal.net

CONTENTS

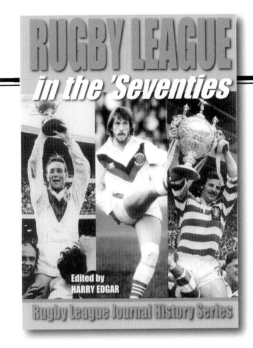

RUGBY LEAGUE in the 'Seventies

Edited by
HARRY EDGAR

Rugby League Journal History Series

Including details of all the tours, World Cups, Test matches, Cup Finals, Championships, Lancashire Cup, Yorkshire Cup, County games, and top scorers.

(Above) Geoff Gunney leads Hunslet's farewell to Parkside in 1973.
(Right) George Nicholls in the 1978 Ashes.
(Below) Malcolm Reilly in Australia in 1970.

The Publisher would like to thank all friends who assist "Rugby League Journal" and whose loan of valuable photographs and items of memorabilia have helped in the compilation of this book. Our thanks also to all the photographers, especially Eddie Whitham and Andrew Varley, whose skills have provided so many fine images - with so many old pictures from private collections it is often difficult to ascertain their origins, thus there has been no intention to breach anybody's copyright.

INTRODUCTION

(Above)
Three of the most outstanding players and finest ambassadors to represent Great Britain during the 'Seventies - George Fairbairn, Steve Nash and Roger Millward, pictured here in action in the 1977 World Cup against France in Auckland. The French scrum-half is Guy Alard. Fairbairn, Nash and Millward played for their country in many epic Test and World Cup games right across the decade.

Welcome to the fourth volume in our *"Rugby League Journal History Series"* in which we take you back to the 'Seventies. Our previous volumes on the 'Fifties and the 'Sixties have been very well received as we set out to provide illustrated guides to the game's history, providing nostalgia for those old enough to have been around to remember those times, and new knowledge for younger generations.

History has come to judge the 1970s as a decade of significant change in Rugby League, when old ways met new and - after periods of turmoil and argument - some desperately needed reorganisation took place. Not all the changes were good, as some valuable traditions were lost in favour of a rather gaudy approach and a lot of what we saw in British Rugby League in the mid-'70s was not pretty. That came as an enormous contrast to the classic style of the Great Britain teams which had won the Ashes in 1970 and the World Cup two years later. But the need to boost morale in the game was paramount and was successfully achieved. What stands out most about Rugby League in the 'Seventies is that there was an incredible amount going on, both domestically and on the international front - and it has been a very difficult task to try and cram everything into this volume. I hope you will enjoy what we have managed to include in this look back at those action packed times.

Harry Edgar (Editor - 'Rugby League Journal')

BRITISH STARS OF THE SEVENTIES

In a decade when many of Britain's best players were enticed to join Australian clubs before an international transfers ban was reintroduced in 1977, the game in the U.K. seemed to have an endless production line of talented footballers. Club teams were almost exclusively made up of home grown players, and the variety of having so many different clubs all vying for honours meant competition for international selection was always intense. And there *was* a heck of a lot of international Rugby League during the 'Seventies for British players to take part in. With three full Lions tours to Australia and New Zealand and no less than four World Cup tournaments, there was hardly time to pause for breath. In addition, throw in two home Ashes series against Australia and a Test series versus New Zealand plus annual internationals against France, either as part of the European Championship involving England and Wales or full Test matches with Great Britain, and you could say the game was suffering from 'international overload.' Not that any of the players were heard complaining, despite all having to earn their livings working full-time in their day jobs.

(Above)
Neil Fox in action for Bradford Northern in 1978, a year in which he enjoyed a fine game against the Australian tourists at Odsal, scoring two tries at the age of 39. One of the game's greatest ever careers, which spanned fully 25 seasons in the senior ranks, came to an end the following year when Neil hung up his boots. On 27th December 1977, as a Huddersfield player, Fox had become the top points scorer in the history of the game, overtaking Jim Sullivan's record of 6,022. Neil Fox went on to register a total of 6,220 points in his magnificent career, and was still a major force in the game throughout the 1970s.

So many of those players gave wonderful service to their country in the international arena. The Ashes winners of 1970 and World Cup winners of 1972 have been give their due place in the history of the game, but the Lions of 1974 and World Cup team of 1977 also deserve far more credit than they have been given as teams who played with great courage and ability in adversity, only to be denied the glory of success by the narrowest of margins. One can only speculate how results may have been different had Great Britain not been denied the services of so many star players who had gone to play for Australian clubs, most notably Malcolm Reilly and Brian Lockwood who were dominating figures of the 'Seventies in both hemispheres. But nothing should ever diminish the contribution made by men like Roger Millward, Steve Nash and George Nicholls who served their country so well throughout the decade.

Whilst the junior game in the northern heartlands of Rugby League was able to keep on supplying so many outstanding players, not least such artistic and creative stand-offs as Ken Gill, John Holmes, David Topliss or Ken Kelly and a whole list of scrum-halves from Reg Bowden to Parry Gordon and Arnold Walker, who always found themselves playing second fiddle to Steve Nash when it came to international selection, British hopes were also boosted by recruits from Rugby Union. In this book you will find a list of all the capped Union internationals who signed for League clubs during the 1970s, but there were several uncapped recruits from the 15-aside game who made a bigger impression in Rugby League, most especially George Fairbairn, John Gray and Mike Nicholas. Gray's rise was meteoric, as he went on tour at the end of his first season with Wigan, became a big star in Sydney, and within a year had returned to live permanently in Australia and play for North Sydney, and later Manly. Scotsman Fairbairn became a Great Britain captain and established himself as the first choice international full-back after taking over from World Cup winner Paul Charlton.

DECADE OF HOPE FOR EVERYONE

(Above)
Blackpool Borough walk out alongside Castleford for the 1977 Players No.6 Trophy final at Salford. Borough's achievement in getting to the final was a great fillip for the "little" clubs in Rugby League.

Above)
Featherstone captain John Newlove scores a try as Rovers won at Wembley in 1973.

The 1970s was a decade when almost every club in the Rugby League had hope of winning something, or at least getting to a major final. Although splitting the league into two divisions was introduced, starting with the 1973-74 season, it was to be several years before the damaging effects of division eventually took its inevitable toll, and several clubs from Division Two were still able to enjoy playing in major finals or semi-finals.

The roll of honour covered such a wider cross section of clubs not just because the game was much more competitive in the 'seventies, but also because there were so many more cup tournaments to play for. In addition to the two biggest targets, the Challenge Cup and the Championship, there were also the two traditional County Cups, and then the BBC Floodlit Trophy, before changes to the league structure and the arrival of sponsorship saw the addition of the Premiership Trophy and the Players No.6 Trophy – plus for one season only, the Captain Morgan Trophy. The Rugby Football League secretary Bill Fallowfield was a keen advocate of more cup competitions and smaller, more intensely contested leagues, as he recognised the spectator pulling-power of games where the result really meant something, as sudden-death knockout games always did.

The variety in the game saw both Leigh and Featherstone Rovers win the Challenge Cup and Dewsbury win the Championship. The latter was a particularly praiseworthy achievement, but it was no fluke for a talented Dewsbury side who also contested a Yorkshire Cup Final and a Floodlit Trophy Final as well as numerous Cup semi-finals. Featherstone Rovers not only won the Challenge Cup in 1973 against

(*Left*) Whitehaven's Gordon Cottier on his way to a try versus Bradford Northern in the 1975 Players No.6 Trophy semi-final - a match which brought the BBC's live television cameras to the Cumbrian club's home ground. (*Below*) Keighley's kicker Brian Jefferson in action against York, he helped to take his team to just one point from Wembley in 1976.

Bradford Northern, they returned to Wembley the following year and then went on to win the Championship in 1977. For a club from a small mining community with a population of no more than 15,000, and a team almost exclusively made up of local lads, it was an incredible achievement. Featherstone, of course, had long been famed as a great Cup fighting side who had already tasted Wembley glory in 1967, so even their achievements in the 'seventies seemed relatively routine compared to Bramley's triumph in the 1973 BBC Floodlit Trophy – always regarded as one of the game's "little" clubs this was a first ever major trophy for the Villagers.

The arrival of the Players No.6 Trophy in 1971-72 saw Halifax become the first winners, and in subsequent years Rochdale Hornets were to get to the Final as did Hull as a Second Division side. Hornets also played in a Floodlit Trophy Final, whilst Swinton, York and Halifax took part in County Cup Finals. The Lancashire Cup became a particular target, and a major galvaniser of support, for Workington Town and they went to four successive finals between 1976 and 1979, winning the trophy in 1977. Matching Bramley's achievement in winning the Floodlit Trophy was Blackpool Borough getting to the Players No.6 Trophy final in 1977 – never was there a more popular underdog in Rugby League than the unsung seaside heroes in tangerine, black and white. And Borough played so bravely in that final against the fast moving Castleford side.

Playing in a Players No. 6 trophy semi-final also presented some of the smaller clubs with a chance to be on live BBC television, as Whitehaven enjoyed at their Recreation Ground in 1975 against Bradford Northern, the eventual winners. But nothing matched the drama of a Challenge Cup semi-final with teams just 80 minutes away from their dream of playing at Wembley – Keighley almost achieved that in 1976 as they scared the life out of St.Helens in a semi-final at Fartown which Saints won by one point, 5-4. Although the quality of the traditionally powerful clubs was always there, it was also a time when every dog could have his day.

(*Above*) **Workington Town enjoy their victory in the 1977 Lancashire Cup Final - Paul Charlton holds the trophy and Billy Pattinson waves to the crowd. It was one of four successive Lancashire Cup Finals in the 'seventies for the Cumbrian club.**

THE CAINE REPORT CONTROVERSY

A period of intense controversy arrived in Rugby League when John Caine Associates of Manchester were appointed as marketing consultants by the Rugby Football League in 1971 to help advise on how the game could arrest its slide in attendances and boost its commercial viability. Their initial report in October 1971 recommended a smaller governing body at the RFL, instead of the 30 member Council, an urgent need to change what they described as the "slag-heap and drizzle" image of the game, improved facilities for spectators, two divisions, and each individual club to be associated with playing one specific day of the week (in the way Salford, for example, had made a success of playing on Friday nights.) The so called "Caine Report" also suggested: "The style and attitude of the BBC coverage is harmful to the general image of the game." The RFL held a conference in Manchester to discuss the report, after which secretary Bill Fallowfield said the League would arrange a meeting with the BBC.

(Above)
John Caine, whose company became embroiled in heaps of controversy after they were appointed as consultants to the Rugby League in 1971 to advise on the marketing of the game. They quickly found themselves at loggerheads with the RFL secretary Bill Fallowfield.

By December 1971, it was known that John Caine Associates had been paid £3,500 to make their report on Rugby League, but all was not well and the marketing company wrote to all 30 professional clubs complaining that the RFL officials were not co-operating with them, and that they had been told to keep away from the BBC-RFL conference on television policy. The RFL said that the consultants appeared to be going outside their terms of reference, and some clubs did not think they were getting value for money and resented the first report with its reference to a "slag heap and drizzle image." But with the successful Salford chairman Brian Snape – seen as the leader of the reformists - having increased influence over the Rugby League Council, John Caine met the management committee and expressed himself as very happy afterwards. He said: "The points we made in our letter to the club chairmen were accepted and we are not thinking of resigning our contract."

By the end of January 1972, the Caine report made further recommendations including the reduction of players in a team from 13 to 11 "to speed up the game and reduce the mauling aspect," as they put it. They also suggested that the Rugby League should make a serious attempt to sell the idea of a family Sunday afternoon going to a Rugby League game; there should be three divisions with a third division of amateur teams; the County Cups should be two-legged affairs up to the final; and there should be a seven-man ruling body with a paid chairman who had no club connection.

(Above)
Eddie Waring, the BBC commentator, whose portrayal of the game made him the target of much of the criticism in the Caine report.

The Rugby League Council turned down the proposals for 11-aside rugby and for three divisions, but accepted the idea of a seven-man ruling body with a paid chairman with no club connection. The Council also agreed to call a special meeting to approve these agreed suggestions from the Caine report, in addition to agreeing that John Caine Associates would handle Rugby League public relations, advertising and publicity.

But just over two months later, things turned full circle and the RFL decided not to renew the contract of John Caine Associates. This prompted one of the game's most experienced and respected journalists, Alfred Drewry of the *'Yorkshire Post'* to write of what he called the *'Caine debacle'*: "They wanted Eddie Waring to change his style, a streamlined governing body in place of the present 30-strong Council, and a multi-division League structure. They also suggested they should handle press relations from their

Manchester office. But the BBC, as far as I am able to judge, still prefer to project Mr. Waring as a comedian, instead of the knowledgeable guide he is, thus setting him apart from the commentators enjoyed by other sports. Signs of the Council being prepared to vote themselves out of office are difficult to detect. Plans for two divisions were turned down at a recent meeting. League headquarters is functioning normally and will continue to do so. All the Caine report has achieved is a lot of hot air and strained tempers. Threats and counter threats of writs are still flying about."

The threatened writs Alfred Drewry was referring to involved the RFL secretary Bill Fallowfield and John Caine – and it was an open secret that Mr. Fallowfield had become a particular target for those frustrated with the way game was presenting itself and, as a result of often strong personal criticism, was determined to defend himself. One of the most vitriolic critics of Fallowfield during the early 1970s was Ken Ashton, then editor of the *'Rugby Leaguer'* weekly newspaper. Ashton was an experienced and quite fearless journalist who made very public his immense frustration with the way the RFL was operating – especially in the 1971-72 season when the game hit its nadir with the home Test series defeat to the Kiwis and at the same time as John Caine Associates were becoming involved with the game. Ken Ashton became a supporter of Caine, and was heavily involved in the new "official magazine" of the RFL published by John Caine Associates and launched in March 1972. *'Rugby Today'* announced itself as being an integral part of the RFL's "policy designed to give Rugby League a brand new image in keeping with the exciting '70s ... to project Rugby League in its true light as one of intense excitement and colour by commissioning a magazine which would be the official voice of Rugby League."

'Rugby Today' duly had an 'Editorial Advisory Board' listed as being made up of leading RFL Council members, including Brian Snape, Tom Mitchell, Robert Massey, Harry Womersley and Ronnie Simpson – plus Alex Murphy, at that time the Warrington player-coach. But very notable by his absence was Bill Fallowfield, which was a clear indicator that the RFL secretary and the game's public mouthpiece for over a quarter of a century was not involved in this self proclaimed "official voice of Rugby League." Some might suggest that Bill had the last laugh as *'Rugby Today'* disappeared after just two issues, whilst he continued for another two seasons at the helm of the game until his retirement in 1974.

The ending of his contract with the RFL in 1972 and the rapid demise of the official magazine he published, did not quite spell the end of John Caine's involvement with the game. In April 1973, Ken Ashton wrote an article glowing in praise of Caine, explaining that his company was still very much part of the scene as marketing consultants for Warrington and the Wilderspool Centre, with Widnes for their centenary celebrations, and with the Lancashire County Rugby League for whom they had obtained a £5,000 sponsorship from Tetley's brewery for the Lancashire Cup. Ken Ashton claimed that many of the suggestions put forward in the "Caine report" were now, in 1973, being acted upon by the RFL, coming to the conclusion that: "The Rugby League could well rue the day certain of its officials found they didn't see eye-to-eye with the Manchester whiz-kid of commerce. Time may well prove that what Caine preached yesterday will be the gospel tomorrow."

(Above)
Brian Snape, the Salford chairman pictured with the Championship trophy. In his role on the Rugby League Council, Mr. Snape became the articulate spokesman for the 'reformists' in the 1970s, and was a key figure in revitalising the game as the decade progressed.

(Above)
Bill Fallowfield, the secretary of the RFL who did not welcome the involvment of John Caine's company.

TIMELINE
1970

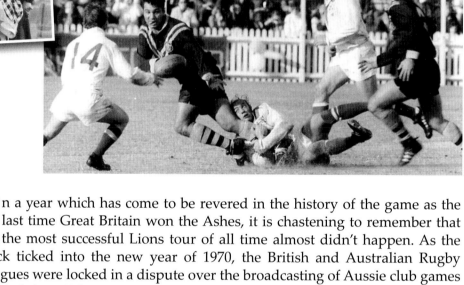

(Above)
The Ashes come home to Britain as the 1970 Lions step off the 'plane at Manchester airport lead by coach Johnny Whiteley and manager Jack Harding.
(Right)
How those 1970 Ashes were won on the Sydney Cricket Ground as the classic tackling of Jimmy Thompson brings Arthur Beetson down watched by Roger Millward and Cliff Watson.

In a year which has come to be revered in the history of the game as the last time Great Britain won the Ashes, it is chastening to remember that the most successful Lions tour of all time almost didn't happen. As the clock ticked into the new year of 1970, the British and Australian Rugby Leagues were locked in a dispute over the broadcasting of Aussie club games on Yorkshire Television. The Rugby Football League were desperate not to upset the BBC, and claimed showing the Australian games on I.T.V. would undermine their own bargaining postion with the BBC in which exclusivity was a major factor. And there's no doubt the BBC were concerned that the way the Australian games were presented did not fit in with the kind of image they seemed anxious to portray for Rugby League. Threats to pull out of the tour seemed very real until, thankfully, the Australian R.L. chairman Bill Buckley managed to settle their differences with the British R.L. secretary Bill Fallowfield.

Despite the success of the Great Britain team on the 1970 tour, the game at home seemed to be locked in turmoil, with one dispute after another as club officials grappled with the financial pressures caused by falling attendances. A switch to Sunday games was gathering momemtum, but not everybody liked it and numerous clubs faced problems with their players refusing to play on Sundays. And there was constant debate over a restructure of the league to include two divisions. Bill Fallowfield was always a supporter of the idea of two divisions, but the clubs themselves could not come up with the necessary two-thirds majority vote at the Rugby League Council to make it happen.

ELSEWHERE IN THE WORLD OF SPORT IN 1970

* Brazil win the football World Cup staged in Mexico, with Pele the star as they beat Italy 4-1 in the final at the Aztec Stadium.
* Substitutes are allowed for the first time which has a direct bearing on holders England's exit from the 1970 World Cup - 2-0 up against West Germany in the quarter-final, Bobby Charlton is substituted and the game turns - West Germany winning 3-2.
* Muhammed Ali comes back for his first fight in four years after been stripped of his world heavyweight title - and stops Don Quarry in three rounds.
* Lester Piggott rode his fifth Derby winner on Nijinski, who went on to be a Triple Crown winner.
* Tony Jacklin, 25, became the first English golfer to win the U.S. Open title for fifty years.

As the arguments over two divisions raged, a sign of changing times came in 1970 when the Lancashire and Yorkshire League Championships were awarded for the last time – for 62 years the county trophies had been a key ingredient of the famous "all four cups," and the last two recipients at the end of the 1969-70 season were Wigan and Leeds. Another change in the governance of the game was the Rugby Football League's decision to have its Chairman of the Council stay *in situ* for two seasons rather than just one, which had been the tradition since the birth of the game. The feeling was that more continuity was required in such challenging times, and the first Chairman to serve the two year period was Hubert Lockwood of Huddersfield, from 1970 to 1972. One of first concerns for the new Chairman was the number of approaches to British players from Australian clubs during the successful Lions tour, with Mick Shoebottom, Syd Hynes and Alan Hardisty among the first to be tempted. In the event, no requests for clearances were received by the British Rugby League and they said these would only be granted in exceptional circumstances.

The Rugby Football League's annual general meeting in June 1970 reported a financial surplus of £15,876, and it was decided to give £600 to each club. More welcome news came when record profits for the Lions tour were announced later in the year, and after each player received a record £790, the RFL decided to share all of the rest among the clubs, with each getting around £1,400. Alas, so much of that feel good factor generated by such a great tour was undone by the World Cup, staged in England just a couple of months after the return of the Lions. Great Britain were hot favourites after the way they had demolished the Australians in the second and third Tests downunder, but it all went pear shaped in the World Cup Final at Headingley. Violence at the end of that final brought the game some unpleasant headlines, and generally low attendances meant that a television fee of £25,000 from the BBC was needed to save the World Cup from making a loss.

The financial concerns of many clubs, set alongside the constant arguing over fixture formats and television, continued to grow and, as the year 1970 approached its close, the now infamous statement from the Hull K.R. director Ron Chester was made: "To say the game is dying is ridiculous. It's dead. When professional clubs are drawing 200 to 300 spectators, the game's gone. The time has passed when TV fees compensated for the disastrous effect the medium had on gates and every effort must be made to negotiate out of the present BBC contract." Future years would show that quite the opposite happened.

(Above) **Wigan's Kevin O'Loughlin is challenged by Whitehaven's Mike Gracey and Barry Buchanan in a replay of the 1970 top-16 play-off first round. Whitehaven caused a big shock to knock out Wigan, the Challenge Cup finalists.**

TOP TEN

1969-70

TRIES
38 J. Atkinson (Leeds)
36 F. Wilson (St.Helens)
33 L. Jones (St.Helens)
31 D. Hill (Wigan)
25 K. Davies (Workington Town)
25 S. Hynes (Leeds)
24 R. Millward (Hull K.R.)
24 M. Shoebottom (Leeds)
24 K. Slater (Wakefield Trinity)
24 C. Sullivan (Hull)

GOALS
167 C. Tyrer (Wigan)
161 K. Coslett (St.Helens)
126 R. Dutton (Widnes)
115 R. Millward (Hull K.R.)
111 T. Price (Bradford Northern)
107 K. Gowers (Swinton)
107 D. Whitehead (Oldham & Warrington)
103 J. Maloney (Hull)
100 P. Donnelly (Whitehaven)
 90 R. Dewhurst (Bramley)
 90 M. Redfearn (Castleford)

TIMELINE 1971

Strange things happened in Rugby League during 1971 as New Zealand ruled the world at international level and Leigh won the Challenge Cup, making it a good year for the underdog. The Kiwis beat all their rivals – Australia, Great Britain and France – but their tour to England, despite some wonderfully entertaining football, revealed the deep problems the game was facing in the country where it was born. A total combined attendance of little more than 13,000 for the three Great Britain versus New Zealand Test matches in the autumn of 1971 was the nadir of the international game, and did much to fans the flames of unrest which would eventually burst into almost open warfare. The RFL found themselves under heavy criticism from some critics for their failure to promote the game and for not appointing a coach to the Great Britain team. Earlier, in April 1971, the RFL had appointed a team of marketing consultants to suggest ways to improve attendances, but their eventual recommendations only provoked more trouble for Bill Fallowfield and the Rugby League Council.

One place where there were no worries about falling crowds was Leigh, where player-coach Alex Murphy built a winning side that would go all the way to Wembley. Under the mercurial Murphy, Hilton Park packed in 10,331 for their first round cup win over Bradford Northern and then 14,649 for the third round against Hull. At Wembley for the first time, Leigh were underdogs against Leeds but dominated them to win the Challenge Cup in the Leythers' finest hour. Leeds were unfortunate to be missing three of their internationals stars because of injuries: Alan Smith, Ray Batten and Mick Shoebottom – the latter had been seriously injured just a couple of weeks earlier as Leeds played Salford in the Championship play-offs at Headingley. Tragically, Shoebottom's injury not only ended his career but had a profound effect on the rest of his life. It was a terrible loss to Leeds and to the game.

The fears that some of Britain's top players would be signed by Australian clubs, which first circulated on the 1970 tour, proved real in February 1971 when Malcolm Reilly left Castleford and emigrated to Australia. The loose-forward played for Cas' in a first round cup-tie at Whitehaven then

(Above)
The fateful moment for Mick Shoebottom as he was injured playing for Leeds versus Salford in 1971.

(Above) Roy Christian, captain of the 1971 New Zealand touring team, is chaired from the field by joyous team-mates after the Kiwis clinched the series against Great Britain by winning the second Test at Castleford. One of the major media talking points about this Kiwi team was that their captain was a direct descendent of Fletcher Christian of "Mutiny on the Bounty" fame.

(Above) Bob Haigh, the Leeds second-rower, who finished joint top try scorer in the 1970-71 season. Haigh scored 40 tries and it was the first time ever a forward had been the game's top try scorer.

jumped on a 'plane to Sydney, where he eventually signed for Manly after Castleford agreed to grant him clearance in exchange for a £15,000 transfer fee and first claim on his services if he returned to England. Reilly was the first of many British stars who headed for Sydney in the early 'seventies. That meant the 1970 World Cup Final had been Reilly's last appearance for Great Britain, and the international team fared little better without him in their first Test of 1971, losing 16-8 against France in Toulouse. Britain got their revenge with an easy 24-2 win over France, with a scrum-half called Steve Nash making his Test debut, in a Wednesday night game at St.Helens televised on the BBC's "Sportsnight" programme, before the shock defeats at the hands of the Kiwis followed later in the year.

Welshman John Mantle covers French centre Michel Molinier as Great Britain lost 16-8 at Toulouse in February 1971.

TOP TEN

1970-71
TRIES
40 **R. Haigh** (Leeds)
40 **L. Jones** (St.Helens)
36 **J. Atkinson** (Leeds)
33 **K. Slater** (Wakefield Trinity)
33 **C. Sullivan** (Hull)
33 **S. Wright** (Wigan)
27 **F. Wilson** (St.Helens)
25 **S. Hynes** (Leeds)
23 **M. Richards** (Salford)
23 **A. Smith** (Leeds)
23 **D. Topliss** (Wakefield Trinity)

GOALS
193 **K. Coslett** (St.Helens)
166 **S. Ferguson** (Leigh)
159 **J. Holmes** (Leeds)
155 **D. Watkins** (Salford)
141 **C. Tyrer** (Wigan)
134 **N. Stephenson** (Dewsbury)
114 **T. Clawson** (Hull K.R.)
110 **N. Fox** (Wakefield Trinity)
99 **F. Davies** (Huddersfield)
98 **B. Jefferson** (Keighley)

TIMELINE
1972

Nothing in 1972 could match the achievement of the Great Britain team in winning the World Cup in France, but whilst Clive Sullivan's side wrote their names into the game's history books as the third British team to win the World Cup, they came home to an almost anonymous welcome as Rugby League's inner turmoil continued. The year got off to an embarrassing start when the Challenge Cup first round draw (being shown live on BBC Television) was bungled after a ball appeared to be dropped on the floor. A re-draw was done, provoking protests from clubs which lost home games. Meanwhile controversies created by the RFL's appointment of John Caine Associates to handle their public relations grew stronger, with the League's secretary Bill Fallowfield becoming a particular target. By April of 1972 the RFL decided to dispense with the services of John Caine's company.

(Above)
Great Britain's 1972 World Cup winners do a lap of honour with the trophy after their heroic final effort against Australia in Lyon. Chris Hesketh and Paul Charlton are the men holding the cup.

Problems were mounting at Hunslet where the sale of their Parkside ground was looking inevitable and, with that, the probable demise of one of the game's most famous old clubs. And the Rugby League Council still could not get its required majority to vote for a switch to two divisions, instead they voted – by a margin of 26-3 - in March 1972 to revert back to the old way of clubs playing all in their own county plus three from the other county, with Dewsbury agreeing to act as a Lancashire club to balance up the numbers. It proved to be smart move by Dewsbury as they went on to win the Championship at the end of the 1972-73 season.

Sponsorship arrived in a major way for Rugby League with the John Player company backing a new mid-season knockout tournament branded

ELSEWHERE IN THE WORLD OF SPORT IN 1972

* The world was horrified as 11 Israeli athletes were murdered by Arab terrorists at the Munich Olympics.
* The Rugby Union Five Nations tournament was abandoned when Scotland and Wales refused to travel to Ireland due to increasing terrorism threats.
* Rugby Union increased the value of a try to four points, from three, in the hope of more open play.
* West Germany became football's European champions for the first time, beating Russia 3-0 in the final played at the Heysel Stadium in Brussels.
* Scottish boxer Ken Buchanan contoversially lost his world lightweight title to Panama's Roberto Duran in New York, following a low blow in the 13th round.
* Cyclist Eddy Merckx of Belgium gains a record equalling fourth consecutive Tour de France victory.

(Above) **Delight for St.Helens as John Mantle holds the Cup after their 1972 Wembley triumph.**

the Players No.6 Trophy. The inaugural competition climaxed in January 1972, with Halifax winning the first final 22-11 against Wakefield Trinity at Odsal Stadium. The key to this sponsorship support was that the competition was to receive national television coverage on the BBC. Further sponsorship followed when the 1972 Lancashire Cup was supported by the brewers Tetley's.

A much changed Great Britain side put behind them the disappointments of losing to the Kiwis in the autumn of 1971, by achieving a home and away double over France early in 1972, winning 10-9 in Toulouse and 45-10 at Bradford. This British team would form the nucleus of the side that went on to win the World Cup later in the year. On the field a major rule change came the start of the 1972-73 season when the six-tackle rule was introduced after being successfully tried in Australia, however the World Cup was played under the previous four-tackle rule as both France and New Zealand felt they had not enough time to adapt to the new rule.

(Above) **Halifax celebrate becoming the very first winners of the new Players No.6 Trophy in January 1972. Skipper Gordon Baker holds the new trophy aloft at Odsal.**

Not long after Great Britain's World Cup triumph, the British game got a glimpse into the future when the Australian Highschools team came on tour for the first time. They ripped all their opposition apart with a stunning brand of high-speed rugby. Meanwhile the RFL tried to help bridge the gap between schools and open-age rugby by introducing a Colts League in 1972.

One player who enjoyed a real Indian summer to his career in 1972 was Frank Foster, the man with the legendary tough-guy image throughout the 'sixties, was signed by Oldham from Barrow in January 1972 and went on to revolutionise their performances. Frank also captained his native Cumberland in their last year of competition before the new county of Cumbria was introduced, and led them to a famous victory over Yorkshire in September 1972 with a performance which prompted the Yorkshire County president, Roy Hartner, to say: "Very ordinary players look seven feet tall when they put a Cumberland jersey on. It is time we put a bit of pride back into playing for Yorkshire."

Despite the much publicised financial pressures facing Rugby League clubs, some were still happy to offer huge inducements to Rugby Union players to switch codes. In late 1972 Wigan reported that the Welsh winger and British Lions star John Bevan had accepted, then returned, their cheque for £12,000. Bevan later claimed he had never received the cheque. And Swinton paid Welsh scrum-half "Chico" Hopkins £8,000 to sign for them.

(Above) **Frank Foster in Oldham's colours as he provided a huge boost to the Roughyeds in 1972.**

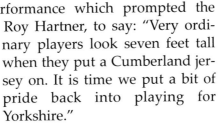

1971-72
TRIES
36 **J. Atkinson** (Leeds)
36 **M. Lamb** (Bradford Northern)
35 **M. Richards** (Salford)
33 **C. Sullivan** (Hull)
30 **D. Watkins** (Salford)
27 **D. Brown** (Widnes)
27 **A. Hardisty** (Leeds)
24 **D. O'Neill** (Widnes)
24 **D. Topliss** (Wakefield Trinity)
23 **M. Elliott** (Oldham)
23 **M. Stephenson** (Hull K.R.)

GOALS
214 **K. Coslett** (St.Helens)
193 **D. Watkins** (Salford)
173 **E. Tees** (Bradford Northern)
120 **T. Clawson** (Hull K.R. & Leeds)
120 **R. Dutton** (Widnes)
119 **K. Gowers** (Swinton)
116 **C. Tyrer** (Wigan)
114 **P. Larder** (Oldham)
108 **J. Maloney** (Hull & York)
108 **D. Whitehead** (Warrington)

After years of debate, in 1973 the Rugby League Council finally voted in favour of splitting the league into two divisions, with 16 clubs in the first division and 14 in the second. One of the clinching factors in getting the approval for this scheme was the ruling that the levy would increase to 15% and be applied to first division games only – a move designed to soften the financial blow for those clubs in the second division and shorn of fixtures against the top teams. The new two divisional scheme kicked off with the 1973-74 season. Before that happened the game's governing body was faced with another problem when a new organisation was born in March 1973 with the aim of taking over control of the amateur side of the game. The British Amateur Rugby League Association was made up of people concerned that the junior side of the game was declining at an alarming rate, and who hoped they could form a body which could stop that downward spiral. However, the Rugby Football League refused to recognise the new amateur association, and secretary Bill Fallowfield issued a statement which said that any club, official or player connected with it would be barred from receiving any benefit from the RFL. It led to a period of bitter dispute for control of the amateur game during 1973, but the organisation which came to be known as BARLA continued to gather momentum.

(Above)
Featherstone Rovers captain John Newlove with his victorious team after the 1973 Cup Final at Wembley.

1973 was the year when Bill Fallowfield started what was to be his last season as secretary of the Rugby Football League after 27 years in the job. It was also the year the original Hunslet club folded and played its last game at Parkside against York on 21st April 1973. Geoff Gunney captained Hunslet onto the field and was the last man to leave it. And it was the year when Great Britain relinquished the Ashes to Australia, never to be seen again in the

ELSEWHERE IN THE WORLD OF SPORT IN 1973

* Sunderland become the first team playing in the second division since the war to win the F.A.Cup, beating Leeds United 1-0 in the final at Wembley.
* Red Rum beats Crisp to win the Grand National.
* Welsh fly-half Barry John retires from Rugby Union at the age of only 27.
* George Foreman becomes world heavyweight champion after knocking out Joe Frazier in the second round in a shock result in Kingston, Jamaica.
* The Wimbledon tennis championships are thrown into chaos when 69 players boycott the event.
* England fail to qualify for the 1974 football World Cup after only managing a Wembley draw with Poland - whose goal-keeping hero Tomaszewski had been labelled 'a clown' by Brian Clough.

(Above) **More big personalities came into Rugby League in 1973. Wigan made headlines when they introduced their new signing from South Africa, Green Vigo, and Salford caused a stir by signing the England Rugby Union winger Keith Fielding. Both were to make an instant impact in League as try-scoring wingers and crowd pleasers.**

(Above) **The President of the Rugby League, Lord Derby and the League's Vice-Chairman Brian Snape, accompanied by Bill Fallowfield, are introduced to the Dewsbury players by captain Mick Stephenson before the 1973 Championship Final.** *(Above right)* **In the autumn of the same year, Bill joined Prime Minister Edward Heath in meeting referee Billy Thompson and the teams before the first Ashes Test at Wembley. By the end of the 1973-74 season, both Mr. Fallowfield and Mr. Heath were no longer in office.**

mother country. Britain could so easily have wrapped the Ashes up in the first two Tests, but fell to the Aussies on a frozen pitch at Warrington in the decider, at the conclusion of a Kangaroo tour which lost money and drew criticism from the Aussies about poor planning, poor promotion, and a general lack of enterprise from the British Rugby League.

(Left) **Arthur Keegan - led Bramley to the Floodlit Trophy.**

The swing away from Saturday afternoon rugby was increasing, and the fixtures for 1973-74 season revealed over 200 league games in the new two division format were scheduled for Sundays, whilst both Salford and St.Helens were playing their home games on Friday nights. But it was certainly a time when the "little" clubs could enjoy success at the highest level, as Featherstone Rovers won the Challenge Cup beating Bradford Northern (who finished 23rd in the league) at Wembley in the final; Dewsbury won the Championship; and Bramley won the BBC2 Floodlit Trophy. Bramley's success came during a winter of power cuts which forced them to play their Floodlit Trophy games in daylight hours.

It was ironic that at a time of such austerity in Rugby League, clubs were speculating bigger money than ever on players – as the trickle of top British stars to Australia started to become a flood, with internationals Bill Ashurst and Mick Stephenson being signed by the Penrith club for £15,000 and a world record £20,000 respectively, the British clubs seemed anxious to make up for it by spending big on men from Rugby Union. Salford signed the Moseley and England winger Keith Fielding, whilst Warrington were the club who finally got Welsh wing star John Bevan. Wigan delighted their fans with the capture of the wonderfully named Green Vigo, who made an instant impact in their televised Sevens tournament before the start of the season, and also picked a winner with their signing of John Gray, a hooker from Coventry Rugby Union Club. Gray was not a big name when Wigan signed him but he proved to be a natural for Rugby League and went on tour with the Great Britain team at the end of his first season in the game.

TOP TEN

1972-73

TRIES
39 J. Atkinson (Leeds)
38 M. Richards (Salford)
33 P. Charlton (Salford)
30 D. Topliss (Wakefield Trinity)
29 P. Lowe (Hull K.R.)
28 A. Hardisty (Leeds)
28 A. Smith (Leeds)
27 G. Dunn (Hull K.R.)
27 D. Redfearn (Bradford Northern)
26 R. Mathias (St.Helens)
26 N. Stephenson (Dewsbury)

GOALS
221 D. Watkins (Salford)
162 K. Coslett (St.Helens)
160 E. Tees (Bradford Northern)
149 N. Stephenson (Dewsbury)
139 C. Kellett (Featherstone Rovers)
138 N. Fox (Wakefield Trinity)
136 D. Whitehead (Warrington)
127 P. Larder (Oldham)
120 B. Jefferson (Keighley)
108 S. Quinn (York)

TIMELINE 1974

This was the year which saw a major changing of the guard in British Rugby League as Bill Fallowfield retired from his position a secretary of the Rugby Football League after 28 years service. It would be unfair to blame Mr. Fallowfield for all the game's problems during the mounting unrest and in-fighting which had bedevilled it throughout the first few years of the 'seventies, but there's no doubt a change in direction was needed to re-energise the game's leadership. That came from the appointment of Brian Snape as Chairman of the Rugby League Council at the start of the 1974-75 season – the man who had successfully revitalised his own Salford club would prove to be the driving force in arresting the game's declining fortunes. And it was Mr. Snape who finalised the appointment of David Oxley as the RFL's new secretary in succession to Bill Fallowfield, from an initial field of 50 applicants for the job of whom eight were interviewed. Oxley, aged 36, was a native of Hull and a deputy headmaster at a school in Dover before he commenced his duties with the Rugby League in July 1974. One of the criteria for the new appointment was that he had to be under 45 years of age.

(Above) **New man at the RFL - David Oxley in 1974.**

![Warrington trophy photo]

(Above) **1974 was a great year for Warrington and their player-coach Alex Murphy. The Wire won the Challenge Cup, the John Player Trophy, the Captain Morgan Trophy and the new Club Championship trophy - being held aloft by Alex in this picture.**

In the final months of his long tenure at the RFL, one of the major problems Bill Fallowfield had to deal with was the growing disputes British clubs were having with their Australian counterparts as they tried to lure our best players down-under. Phil Lowe was the latest, following such as Bishop, Watson, Ashurst, Reilly and Stephenson, and the Hull K.R. second-rower had left to join the Manly club in Sydney without a clearance, causing a major row between the two governing bodies. Amid all this, the British Rugby League had to get ready to send a Lions touring team to Australia and New Zealand, and despite the loss of so many players things seemed to be shaping up nicely before another hammer blow came with the withdrawal of captain-elect Doug Laughton. The Widnes loose-forward had skippered Great Britain to two very convincing Test wins over France early in 1974, at Grenoble and Wigan, and was a sure bet to be named tour captain when he announced he was accepting a lucrative offer from the Canterbury-Bankstown club. The Widnes club were developing a twinning arrangement with Canterbury and had given their approval to Doug spending the summer playing for them. In the event, Laughton's stint in Sydney football was short-lived and his absence opened the way for Chris Hesketh to be appointed the Lions captain, and he proved to be an admirable leader.

Salford's new winger Keith Fielding finished his debut season as top of the try-scoring charts and in his Test debut for Great Britain against France in Grenoble scorched in for a hat-trick, which brought him the nickname of *Le Rapide* from the French press. Fielding had been one of six Salford players selected for the tour, but withdrew for family reasons to be replaced by Rochdale Hornets' John Butler, soon to become a Salford player himself. Fielding's try scoring played a big part in Salford's success in winning the Championship, the first under the new two divisional system of first past the post. When it came to knockout cups, 1974 was Warrington's year – under the guidance of player-coach Alex Murphy, the Wire won at Wembley for the first time in 20 years, and also added the Players No.6 Trophy and two competitions which proved to be one-year wonders in 1974 – the Club Championship and the Captain Morgan Trophy.

As the 1974-75 season kicked off, the first under the RFL's new regime, only Leeds, Wigan and Bramley still wanted to play home games on Saturdays, with everybody else opting for Sundays or Friday nights. Another key recruit came in October 1974 when David Howes, a young journalist from Hull, was appointed as the Rugby League's first public relations officer. Already a new wave optimism was being felt across the game, and as 1974 drew to a close, Chairman Brian Snape stated: "We are an old game and there are too many old men in it. The young men have got to lead the way." That was a reference to a panel of coaches and referees which had been set up to advise on rule

changes and trying to improve the game. A nice moment had come in March of 1974 when Clive Sullivan, the World Cup winning captain of two years earlier, became an M.B.E. - although the behind the scenes disputes had still not gone away as, even before the end of its first season, both Halifax and Swinton were calling for two divisions to be scrapped in favour of a return to regional rugby.

(Above) **Former Great Britain captain Bill Holliday leads Rochdale Hornets out for the 1974 Players No.6 Trophy Final versus Warrington at Wigan.**

(Above)
The 1974 British Lions touring team wave to the camera on picture day at Headingley before setting off for Australia.

TOP TEN

1973-74
TRIES
49 K. Fielding (Salford)
40 R. Mathias (St.Helens)
38 D. Smith (Wakefield Trinity)
26 D. Eckersley (St.Helens)
26 R. Fleay (Swinton)
25 L. Jones (St.Helens)
25 F. Wilson (St.Helens)
24 D. Watkins (Salford)
23 J. Atkinson (Leeds)
23 M. Lamb (Bradford Northern)

GOALS
183 D. Watkins (Salford)
168 D. Whitehead (Warrington)
165 B. Jefferson (Keighley)
134 K. Coslett (St.Helens)
131 K. Mumby (Bradford Northern)
129 R. Dutton (Widnes)
121 G. Lloyd (Castleford)
112 S. Quinn (York)
111 J. Fiddler (Leigh)
107 W. Holliday (Rochdale Hornets)

TIMELINE
1975

(Above)
Widnes began a long run of Wembley Finals when they won the Challenge Cup in 1975 - captained and coached by local boys Doug Laughton and Vince Karalius. They had just beaten Warrington in 1975.

Great progress was made in improving Rugby League's profile, to say nothing of its morale, during 1975, and three particular innovations played a key role in that. By far the most important was the official recognition of BARLA as the national governing body of amateur Rugby League; alongside that came the establishment of a new, revamped Coaching Scheme and the reintroduction of the game to Wales. BARLA had made remarkable progress since its formation in the spring of 1973 – Brian Snape wasted little time as soon as he became Chairman of the RFL in 1974 in giving recognition to BARLA and in 1975 it completed its full recognition by the Central Council for Physical Recreation. In March 1975 BARLA took control of Great Britain's amateur internationals for the first time. The new Coaching Scheme was headed by Albert Fearnley and Laurie Gant, with five regional coaches – Graham Starkey (Lancashire), Arthur Bunting (Humberside), Jack Scroby and Garth Budge (Yorkshire) and Ron Morgan (Cumbria) working under them.

The reformation of a Welsh national team was part of the RFL new regime's plans to increase the profile of the sport via international competition. The European Championship was reintroduced in the early months of 1975 as the familiar triangular tournament between England, France and Wales, but a new innovation allowed the Welsh to include a small number of "heritage" players to help ensure it had

ELSEWHERE IN THE WORLD OF SPORT IN 1975

* Leeds United lose 2-0 to Bayern Munich in the European Cup Final, after which English 'fans' riot and Leeds are banned from Europe for three years.
* British motorbiker Barry Sheene shocks world champion Giacomo Agostini to win the Dutch TT Grand Prix, but the Italian recovers to win his eighth 500-cc world championship.
* Niki Lauda in a Ferrari holds off Britain's James Hunt to win the world motor-racing championship.
* Muhammad Ali beats Joe Bugner on points after 15 rounds in searing heat in Kuala Lumpar.
* Clive Lloyd hits 102 runs as West Indies beat Australia in the final of cricket's world cup.

(Left)
Hull Kingston Rovers winger Ged Dunn was the game's top try-scorer in the 1974-75 season and continued his scoring form for England in the 1975 World Championships with this try against New Zealand at Odsal. John Holmes is the man in support.

(Above)
George Fairbairn with England in 1975.

quality in all positions. What nobody had expected was that the Rugby League would take the bold step of staging a major game in Wales – for the first time in over 20 years. It was a shot in the dark to guess what sort of reaction the Welsh public would provide for a match against France at Swansea on a Sunday afternoon in February 1975, but the reality was overwhelming as so many spectators were still queuing to get in some 15 minutes after the kick off that the gates were opened and several thousand got in free. Nobody knew exactly how big the crowd was, but estimates ranged anywhere between 10,000 and 20,000 – what was indisputable was the wonderful welcome they gave to returning Welsh heroes like David Watkins and John Bevan.

That success in Swansea was a real landmark day for Rugby League in 1975. One of the spin offs was that the Rugby League opened ticket offices in Cardiff and Swansea for the Challenge Cup Final and reported it to be a big success. And the feelgood factor continued with a rousing match at Wembley which saw Widnes triumph against neighbours Warrington and provide a much needed contrast to some of the unpleasantness which had marred the 1974 Cup Final. It was the first of many Wembley Cup Finals for Widnes which would earn them the reputation of being Cup Kings.

A massive international innovation in 1975 was a World Championship involving a series of matches in both hemispheres and spanning two different seasons. Wales and England played separately, making it a five team tournament with Australia, New Zealand and France – with media spice added by making Alex Murphy the England coach. Taking advantage of the new "heritage" selection criteria introduced to help the Welsh, England were able to include the Scotsman George Fairbairn, a talented 19-year-old who had made an immediate impression after signing for Wigan from the Borders. And the English team broke new ground for international Rugby League when they travelled to play Papua New Guinea at the nation's capital Port Moresby on 5th July, England winning 40-12 and becoming the first European side to experience the unique conditions of playing in P.N.G.

TOP TEN

1974-75

TRIES
42 G. Dunn (Hull K.R.)
35 K. Fielding (Salford)
31 J. Bevan (Warrington)
30 R. Millward (Hull K.R.)
30 A. Smith (Leeds)
29 J. Atkinson (Leeds)
28 M. Richards (Salford)
28 C. Sullivan (Hull)
27 R. Mathias (St.Helens)
26 L. Dyl (Leeds)

GOALS
146 N. Fox (Hull K.R.)
129 K. Coslett (St.Helens)
122 R. Dutton (Widnes)
112 G. Lloyd (Castleford)
112 S. Quinn (York)
110 J. Hartley (Huddersfield)
107 I. MacCorquodale (Workington)
107 D. Marshall (Leeds)
 96 K. Mumby (Bradford Northern)
 85 J. Fiddler (Leigh & Salford)

TIMELINE 1976

The new year of 1976 started in fine style for Rugby League when Chris Hesketh, captain of Salford and the 1974 Lions touring team, was awarded an M.B.E. – making him the fourth player from the sport to be so honoured, his predecessors being Eric Ashton, Geoff Gunney and Clive Sullivan. And Hesketh had another very successful year on the pitch as he guided the Red Devils to their second Championship title in three seasons. Salford had the notable distinction of both their wingers, Maurice Richards and Keith Fielding, finishing as the top two in the try-scoring charts, with a fellow former Rugby Union international, David Watkins, topping both the goal and points scoring charts. Salford were the game's most glamorous club, famed for playing sparkling attacking rugby under floodlights at The Willows, where they became known for attracting celebrities in the audience. But for all their quality, the Red Devils continued to be frustrated when it came to winning the knockout trophies which, alas for them, brought far more attention and acclaim than the Championship.

(Above)
Keighley defenders get to grips with St.Helens in the 1976 Cup semi-final at Fartown. Keighley finished just one point away from a Wembley Cup Final.

Instead it was St.Helens who picked up the silverware, winning the Challenge Cup in 1976 and making it a "double" when they also won the Premiership Trophy – beating Salford in the final at Swinton. Saints gained special satisfaction from their Wembley victory over Widnes after being taunted about their aging forwards not being able to keep up with the young bulls of the Chemics. Yet, on a scorching hot day at Wembley, the St.Helens pack were dominant and they paved the way for a convincing win against the previous year's Cup holders. The special guest who presented the trophy at Wembley was a young politician on her way up as the new leader of the opposition, the Rt. Hon. Mrs Margaret Thatcher. There was no relaxation for St.Helens after their triumphs at home in a 52 match season, as they became the first British club side to travel to Australia and New Zealand. Saints opening match on Aussie soil was a 21-15 defeat to the Queensland state side in Brisbane, before they moved on to Sydney to play the very first unofficial "world club championship" match against Eastern Suburbs. The Roosters, coached by Jack Gibson and captained by Arthur Beetson, beat St.Helens 25-2.

It was only by the narrowest of margins that Saints actually got to Wembley after they struggled to overcome the challenge of Keighley in the semi-final. It was a remarkable effort by the Yorkshire club to go so far in the Challenge Cup, inspired by the kicking skills of their full-back Brian Jefferson, and they were unlucky to miss out on Wembley by just one point as St.Helens won the semi-final 5-4 at Fartown.

By the end of the 1975-76 season, the RFL's public relations officer David Howes was able to report that League match attendances had gone up by 30,000 – not a lot, he said, but it was significant that things were moving upwards after the problems of earlier years. Not all was hunky dory among the clubs, however, an in May 1976 Bramley proposed a return to one division, but lost the vote 19-10 with the New Hunslet club not represented. That meant at least one third of the League's member clubs still preferred to go back to one division. As BARLA continued to oversee remarkable progress, indeed a revitalisation, in the amateur game, the RFL's own Colts League had

(Above)
The plaque which was installed in 1976 at the George Hotel in Huddersfield to commemorate the birthplace of the game.

become a semi-professional competition with its own Challenge Cup and Championship being contested in 1975-76 – the Wigan Colts winning the double. 1976 also saw the first Colts internationals against France – the opening encounter was a chastening experience for the British as they were hammered 39-5 by the French Juniors in the glamorous surroundings of Cannes, but the British Colts got their revenge a few weeks later by winning 31-12 at Salford. Anglo-French internationals were also revived at Under-24 level, the Great Britain side were captained by Castleford stand-off Bruce Burton and won a double against France, 19-2 at Hull K.R. and 11-9 in a bloodbath at Albi.

(Above) **Salford captain Chris Hesketh, MBE, with the 1976 Championship.**

The spread of amateur Rugby League made national headlines when a club was formed in Oxford, and the city of dreaming spires was also the place where a new publication dedicated to spreading the game was born - the first issue of *"Open Rugby"* was produced there in May 1976. Amid all the new innovations and progress at youth and amateur levels, Rugby League did, at last, pay some homage to its history by installing a commemorative plaque at the game's birthplace, the George Hotel in Huddersfield. The plaque was created by the Yorkshire based designer Geoff Quinn, brother of Steve, the York and Featherstone Rovers goal-kicker.

(Left)
Wigan scrum-half Jim Nulty touches down for the Great Britain Under-24s in their opening win over France at Hull K.R. in 1976.

TOP TEN

1975-76

TRIES
37 M. Richards (Salford)
33 K. Fielding (Salford)
31 L. Jones (St.Helens)
26 W. Briggs (Leigh & Warrington)
26 D. Smith (Wakefield Trinity)
25 B. Burton (Halifax & Castleford)
23 G. Clark (Hull)
22 I. Wright (Workington Town)
21 D. Barends (York)
21 K. Boxall (Hull)
21 J. Butler (Salford)
21 J. Holmes (Leeds)
21 R. Mathias (St.Helens)
20 J. Bevan (Warrington)
20 E. Hughes (Widnes)

GOALS
175 D. Watkins (Salford)
149 G. Lloyd (Castleford)
149 G. Pimblett (St.Helens)
148 R. Dutton (Widnes)
146 G. Fairbairn (Wigan)
137 M. Stacey (Leigh)
130 I MacCorquodale (Workington)
102 N. Fox (Hull K.R. & York)
101 D. Marshall (Leeds)
100 R. Gaitley (New Hunslet)

TIMELINE
1977

(Right)
Widnes scrum-half Reg Bowden moves the ball before John Holmes can tackle him during the 1977 Cup Final at Wembley - in the background are Leeds forwards Phil Cookson and Steve Pitchford.

(Below)
Steve Quinn, whose prolific goal-kicking helped Featherstone Rovers to win the Championship in 1977 for the first time in their history.

There was no more romantic story in 1977 than Blackpool Borough reaching their first major final. The seaside club, who had always been among the game's strugglers, won through to the Players No. 6 Trophy Final, in which they took on mighty Castleford at Salford. By this time, Cas' had established themselves as the outstanding footballing side in the country, inspired by player-coach Malcolm Reilly who had returned from his time in Australia with a dodgy knee, but a wealth of knowledge to go with his already well known skills and competitive attitude. Malcolm was still a great player and had some talented players emerging in his team, not least full-back Geoff Wraith, centre John Joyner and stand-off Bruce Burton. But brave little Blackpool, coached by Jim Crellin, gave them a real game in the January final at The Willows, winning the admiration of everybody in the game.

It was a big year for international Rugby League with yet another World Cup being staged jointly in Australia and New Zealand, with the Great Britain team being reformed to take part as it was again felt Wales could not gather enough players of international quality. That certainly ruffled the Welsh feathers and they took great delight in confounding their critics by beating England 6-2 at Headingley in the opening match of the 1977 European Championship. But that result eventually proved academic for both the home countries as they both were beaten in France. The French were cockahoop at winning the Jean Galia Trophy, beating Wales in Toulouse and then England in a rip-roaring game at Carcassonne in front of a capacity

12,000 crowd. England's coach in these games was Peter Fox, who achieved the remarkable distinction of being chosen as the national team coach whilst in charge of a second division club – Fox guiding Bramley to promotion in 1977. Unfortunately for Peter, who had been a hot favourite to take the Great Britain team down-under for the World Cup, England finishing bottom in the European Championship saw his Welsh counterpart David Watkins given the Great Britain job, even though he had no club coaching expe-

rience. There had been 12 applications for the British coaching job, a list reduced to a shortlist of four: Fox, Watkins, Alex Murphy (Warrington) and Dave Cox (Dewsbury).

(Above) **Castleford's captain-coach Malcolm Reilly lifts the Players No. 6 Trophy in January 1977 as Sammy Lloyd is congratulated by Lord Derby. Reilly's team had just beaten Blackpool Borough in an enjoyable final at The Willows, Salford.**

As things turned out, Great Britain played very well in the World Cup, qualifying for the Final and losing that to Australia in Sydney by just one point. With numerous established internationals missing, several new boys got their chance and played superbly – not least the mighty Leeds prop Steve Pitchford who was a late call up for the team after his magnificent Lance Todd Trophy winning performance at Wembley as Leeds beat Widnes in the best final of the decade to date. But the outstanding club achievement of all was by Featherstone Rovers, who won the Championship title for the first time in their history.

(Above) **David Ward, in his 1977 World Cup suit, receiving his award as the inaugral "Man of Steel."**

In February 1977 British Rugby League saw its first ever 1-nil result in a match between Dewsbury and York – the only score being a drop-goal by Nigel Stephenson. Later in the year Cawoods of Hull became the first amateur team since 1909 to knock out a professional club in a major cup competition when they beat Halifax 9-8 at Thrum Hall. Other "firsts" saw Workington Town win the Lancashire Cup, and BARLA make real sporting history by sending the first amateur team on tour to the southern hemisphere as their Under-18s travelled to Australia and New Zealand. Sponsorship was steadily increasing in the game, and as the 1977-78 season kicked off, the RFL reported a total central sponsorship income of £77,000, plus a new three-year contract with BBC Television has been signed. A new award scheme was launched in 1977 as the Trumanns Man of Steel ceremony was staged in Manchester (Trumanns were a steel-making company), with the first winner being David Ward the Leeds hooker and captain. That was in sharp contrast to the tragedy which struck the Leeds club in April 1977 when their half-back Chris Sanderson died from injuries sustained in a play-off match at Salford.

TOP TEN

1976-77
TRIES

31	S. Wright	(Widnes)
29	B. Burton	(Castleford)
28	D. Smith	(Leeds)
27	K. Fielding	(Salford)
26	E. Cunningham	(St.Helens)
26	G. Dunn	(Hull K.R.)
24	R. Mathias	(St.Helens)
24	D. Topliss	(Wakefield Trinity)
23	M. Richards	(Salford)
22	D. Barends	(York)

GOALS

163	G. Lloyd	(Castleford)
152	G. Pimblett	(St.Helens)
152	S. Quinn	(Featherstone Rovers)
132	S. Hesford	(Warrington)
128	I. MacCorquodale	(Workington)
125	D. Watkins	(Salford)
106	N. Stephenson	(Dewsbury)
105	G. Fairbairn	(Wigan)
97	R. Dutton	(Widnes)
90	J. Woods	(Leigh)

TIMELINE
1978

The progress Rugby League had made in the four years since the new regime took over at Chapeltown Road was immense, and the events of 1978 presented such a positive contrast to the dark days of 1973-74. In the summer of 1978, it was announced that Division One attendances were up by 14% and Division Two by 11%, plus the Challenge Cup Final crowd of 95,872 was a Wembley sell-out for only the third time in the game's history. This prompted the RFL secretary David Oxley to comment: "Morale in the game is sky high. Rugby League is faster and as exciting and skilful as it has ever been." That upward spiral continued when the Australians came on tour in the autumn of 1978 and found a vastly different landscape to the one they had endured on their 1973 tour – big crowds watched many of the Kangaroos' club games and they went home with a sizeable profit. The contrast was perfectly illustrated by the way the deciding third Test in 1978 drew a capacity crowd of 29,627 to Headingley with tickets sold out overnight, compared to 1973 where the deciding third Test drew only 10,019.

(Above)
Widnes centre Mal Aspey dives over for a spectacular try in the 1978 Premiership Final at Swinton as Bradford's David Redfearn gives chase.

A massive landmark came when BARLA sent their first Open Age international touring team to the southern hemisphere – something which had previously been unthinkable for the game's amateur players. An even more remarkable credit to the pioneering achievements of BARLA was that part of their trip was the first major tour by any overseas sporting team to Papua New Guinea. Another overseas adventure which appeared to be gathering pace in 1978 was the plan to start the game in America, headed by Mike Mayer. A launch in New York was attended by top Rugby League officials from around the world.

The Challenge Cup Final between Leeds and St.Helens continued the feelgood momentum of the previous year's showpiece, and turned out to be one of the most exciting and dramatic games ever seen at Wembley. Leeds came back to retain the Cup after Saints had stormed ahead, the Loiners' victory march including a classic winger's try by John

ELSEWHERE IN THE WORLD OF SPORT IN 1978

* Argentina stages the FIFA World Cup and wins it, beating Holland 3-1 in the final in Buenos Aires.
* Scotland's World Cup campaign, under manager Ally MacLeod, fails to live up to their hype.
* Muhammad Ali wins back the world heavyweight title for an historic third time at the age of 37.
* Liverpool win the European Cup for the second year running, whilst Nottingham Forest, under manager Brian Clough, win the championship in their first season after promotion.
* The BBC cover the snooker world championship in full for the first time, as 45-year-old Welshman Ray Reardon becomes the oldest man to win it.
* Martina Navratilova wins her first Wimbledon championship, beating Chris Evert in the final.

Atkinson and late drop-goals by John Holmes and David Ward to put Leeds ahead. However, the drama was not over as St.Helens centre Derek Noonan had a last second chance to win the game, only for the ball to elude him close to the corner flag, after a game which had flowed from end to end.

Widnes won the Championship for the first time in their 105-year history. The Chemics coach Frank Myler also took charge of the England team as they put the disappointments of 1977 behind them and stormed to the European Championship. It was a blow to the Rugby League's hopes of continuing to build the momentum in Wales when their scheduled match against England at Swansea in February had to be called off because of heavy snow. Bradford Northern were runners-up in the First Division, and beat Widnes in the Premiership Final. The Odsal club became the centre of much activity in the game with their Chairman Harry Womersley having taken over from Brian Snape as Chairman of the Rugby League Council, and then being appointed manager of the Great Britain team for the 1978 Ashes series. His Bradford coach Peter Fox (whom they had recruited from Bramley) was named as the Great Britain coach, but he was unable to guide his team to victory over the Australians – unlike the French coach Roger Garrigues who saw his country achieve a surprise two-nil Test series win over the Aussies.

(Above) **Debut try - on 26th November 1978, a teenager called Ellery Hanley played his first senior game for Bradford Northern and scored a try in a 30-18 win over Rochdale Hornets at Odsal. It would prove to be the first of many for young Ellery.**

(Above) **John Atkinson on his way to a classic try at Wembley in 1978 as Leeds came back to win the Cup against St.Helens.**

(Above) **British captain Roger Millward gets a "don't argue" from the Australian prop Craig Young during the second Test of the 1978 Ashes series. Loose-forward Steve Norton covers across.**

TIMELINE
1979

(Right) The Wakefield Trinity half-backs David Topliss and Mike Lampkowski in action against Widnes in the 1979 Challenge Cup Final. Widnes held out to win in their fourth Wembley final in five years.

(Above) 1979 saw Papua New Guinea's first ever tour to Europe.

After all the positive signs in the second half of the 'seventies, British Rugby League got a harsh wake-up call in 1979 when the Lions tour to Australia proved to be a disaster. On the field the team coached by Eric Ashton became the first to lose all three Tests in a series against Australia, and for the Rugby Football League it was a hard financial bullet to bite as the tour lost £31,590 compared with a profit of £93,282 in 1974.

Before the tour all seemed well, and at international level England retained the Jean Galia Trophy as European Champions after overcoming a strong challenge from a French side in confident mood after beating Australia in both Tests at the end of the previous year. That success enabled France to draw their biggest crowd for a long time in their home match against Wales, playing at Narbonne for the first time, with an official attendance of 13,728 paying spectators from an estimated total approaching 20,000. England were captained by the experienced Brian Lockwood, although there was some criticism of the selectors when they said a number of established internationals had been left out of the England side because they wanted to look at other players before choosing the tour squad. This prompted Johnny Whiteley, former Great Britain player and coach of the victorious 1970 touring team, to say: "They have made a mockery of one of the greatest honours in the game. I sweated blood to get

(Above, left) Hull's Vince Farrar raises the Division Two winners trophy after leading the "Airlie Birds" to a record-breaking undefeated season in the league. Hull won all 26 of the games to win promotion as Division Two champions in 1979. *(Above, right)* Featherstone's Steve Evans, playing stand-off, on the attack for England in their 12-6 victory over France at Wilderspool which clinched the European Championship in 1979 - the French players are scrum-half Guy Alard and prop Delphin Castanon.

my England jersey, and fought hard to keep it." The 1979 Cup Final was a landmark event as it marked the 50th anniversary since the Final was first played at Wembley, and in a lovely ceremony the RFL arranged for all surviving members of the Wigan and Dewsbury teams who had played in that first game in 1929 to be introduced to the Wembley crowd. There were memories of the 'sixties as Wakefield Trinity qualified for Wembley, but there was no Cup glory for them – despite captain David Topliss winning the Lance Todd Trophy – as they went down to a Widnes team playing in the fourth Wembley final in five years. Hull Kingston Rovers won the Championship and their neighbours Hull were Second Division champions after a remarkable season in which they won all 26 league games.

As the last season of the decade kicked off, Leeds were the only club left in the Rugby League playing their home games on Saturdays. The commercialisation of the game continued apace with the Challenge Cup being sponsored for the first time by State Express, and an announcement that a three year deal worth £215,000 had been agreed with Slalom Lager to sponsor the first and second divisions and the Premiership. The RFL also announced that the ban on advertising on jerseys was likely to be lifted during the 1979-80 season – ironically that came at the same time the Floodlit Competition was dropped by the BBC. Most clubs' floodlights were not good enough for colour television and it was costing the BBC £9,000 per game to provide extra lighting.

Rugby League fans saw history being made when Papua New Guinea made their first tour to Europe in the autumn of 1979, first travelling to France and then being hosted by BARLA for three games in England.

TOP TEN

1978-79

TRIES

35	S. Hartley	(Hull K.R.)
28	S. Wright	(Widnes)
25	D. Barends	(Bradford Northern)
25	P. Lowe	(Hull K.R.)
25	P. Prendiville	(Hull)
24	K. Fielding	(Salford)
23	D. Redfearn	(Bradford Northern)
22	R. Mathias	(St.Helens)
21	G. Bray	(Hull)
21	Keiron O'Loughlin	(Wigan)
21	C. Sullivan	(Hull K.R.)
20	J. Bevan	(Warrington)

GOALS

172	G. Lloyd	(Hull)
170	S. Hesford	(Warrington)
140	M. Burke	(Widnes)
114	I. MacCorquodale	(Workington)
105	G. Pimblett	(St.Helens)
97	G. Beale	(Doncaster & Keighley)
95	J. Woods	(Leigh)
96	J. Birts	(Halifax)
86	G. Fairbairn	(Wigan)
84	P. Norton	(Castleford)

WEMBLEY KNOCKOUT DRAMAS

(Right)
Castleford scrum-half Keith Hepworth connects with Wigan full-back Colin Tyrer in the 1970 Cup Final.

(Far right)
The referee Billy Thompson points to the dressing-rooms as Leigh players look on at Wembley in 1971, and the Leeds captain Syd Hynes is about to get his marching orders.

W embley has always had its moments of great drama for Rugby League, but the Cup Finals of the early 'seventies provided some of the game's most controversial incidents - truly some knockout moments! It started in 1970 when Castleford scrum-half Keith Hepworth leapt high to meet Wigan full-back Colin Tyrer as he ran the ball out and passed to winger Kevin O'Loughlin in the 18th minute of the first half. Tyrer was left nursing a broken jaw and presented a sorry sight as he was helped from the field with blood tricking from his face. It left Wigan without their star goal-kicker, which certainly counted in such a close game, won eventually by Castleford 7-2. To many people's surprise, the referee Fred Lindop did not send Hepworth off.

In the following year's Cup Final, the referee Billy Thompson took a very different view of an incident involving the rivals skippers Syd Hynes of Leeds and Alex Murphy of Leigh. Few, if any, of the Wembley crowd saw what took place, and certainly the BBC cameras did not pick up the incident, after a flashpoint which left Murphy lying motionless on the ground. After consulting with one of his touch-judges, referee Thompson pointed to the dressing-rooms and Syd Hynes became the first Rugby League player ever to be sent off at Wembley. Murphy was carried to the dressing-rooms apparently unconscious - although he recovered enough to come back and lead his team up to receive the cup. Folklore has it that Murphy winked as he was carried off, but Alex always denied this.

(Above)
Rough justice for Featherstone hooker Keith Bridges as he takes a direct hit from Billy Pickup of Warrington in the 1974 Cup Final.

(*Above*) **Whilst Syd Hynes was getting his marching orders, Alex Murphy was making his own exit from the Wembley stage on a stretcher, carried off appearing to be unconscious.**

Only referee Thompson knew what he saw, and - at the end of the day - only two men know fully what really happened: Murphy and Hynes. Three years later, Alex was back at Wembley, this time leading Warrington to a victory in the 1974 Cup Final against Featherstone Rovers. Murphy himself was lucky not to be more severely punished after a bad high tackle on Dave Hartley early in the game, and the referee Sam Shepherd had a thankless task trying to keep a lid on tempers. When things finally erupted with a mass brawl in the second half, Rovers hooker Keith Bridges was knocked out cold and had to be carried off on a stretcher.

(*Above*)
Syd Hynes makes the long, lonely walk to the dressing-rooms in 1971, the first man to be sent off in a Wembley Cup Final.

CLUB FOUNDATIONS

Away from the high profile of the international arena and Cup finals, the foundations of Rugby League during the 'Seventies were maintained by clubs without much glamour. Here's a glimpse of life at some of the clubs who were not winning major trophies in the 1970s.

DONCASTER LOYALTY

It took a special breed of loyalty to keep Doncaster going as they struggled near the bottom of the Second Division throughout the 1970s. One player who stuck by the Dons was Trevor Denton, pictured in action *(above)* at Tattersfield.

HULL'S AUSSIE INVASION

Hull had an invasion of Aussies in 1972-73, and seven of them are pictured *(above)* with coach Ivor Watts. The most successful was Len Dittmar (far left at the back) who played 18 games; whilst others who made the first team were Mark Willoughby, Bob Shaw and Kevin Tommerup.

WHITEHAVEN FIRST SPONSORS

Whitehaven became the first club to carry a sponsor's name on their jerseys when they were backed by the newly established Copeland Council in the mid-70s. *(Right)* Mayor John Colligan points to the logo on 'Haven' captain John McFarlane's jersey.

OLDHAM'S DREAM

Despite never being afraid to spend big to sign players, Oldham's dream of going to Wembley remain unfulfilled. *(Left)* The Oldham team in the 1973-74 season. Left to right: *(Standing):* Stuart Bottom, Mike Elliott, Brian Gregory, Keith Ashcroft, Tony Peters, Fred Hall, Bill McCracken, John Blair. *(In front):* David Treasure, Martin Murphy, Chris O'Brien, Mick McCone, Kevin Taylor, Phil Larder and Geoff Munro.

THE COLOURFUL WORLD OF RUGBY LEAGUE

Just four examples of the varied artwork of printed documents in the 'Seventies

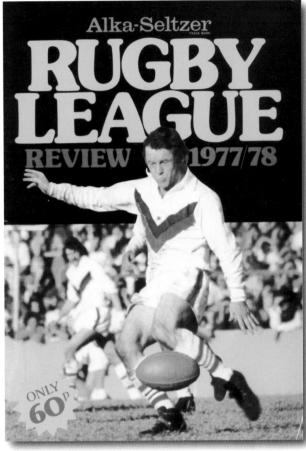

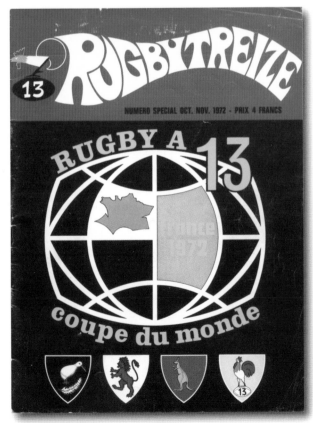

LIONS ON TOUR 1970

Captained by Frank Myler, with Cliff Watson his vice-captain, the 1970 Lions proved to be Great Britain's most successful touring team of all. Not least, of course, they won back the Ashes from Australia for what has proved to be the last time, but they also managed to go through their whole tour losing only one game in Australia (the first Test), drawing one (against New South Wales) and winning every other, including three Tests in New Zealand. This record even managed to surpass the wonderful 1958 touring team, who lost two games, albeit they played six more than the 1970 Lions. The team were managed by Mr. Jack Harding of Leigh and coached by Johnny Whiteley, himself a member of the great 1958 Lions team. Whiteley played a massive role in the success of the 1970 tour, combining his job as coach with being assistant manager, trainer, physiotherapist, kitman and a whole variety of other duties.

For the first time the tour followed a different itinerary in Australia which saw them kick off at Darwin in the Northern Territory and then travel southward through Queensland, playing five games before going into the first Test in Brisbane. This was instead of the previous time honoured tour schedule of playing successive big Saturday games on the Sydney Cricket Ground against Sydney and New South Wales, before going into the first Test at the same venue. After Great Britain were outclassed 37-14 by Australia in that rugged first Test in Brisbane, there was much criticism of the "easy" build up of matches in the sunshine state of Queensland, which did little to prepare the British boys for the intensity of an Ashes Test match.

After their heavy first Test defeat in 1970, coach Whiteley knew changes had to be made to his Test team and a key moment in turning round the tour came in the match against New South Wales. The Lions were losing 15-2, but skipper Frank Myler rallied his troops and inspired them to recover for a 17-all draw as they put the foundations in place for the second Test seven days later. Great Britain's much changed side hammered the Aussies 28-7, with Roger Millward in at stand-off and equalling the Ashes Test individual record of 20 points. New forwards Dennis Hartley, Tony Fisher and Jimmy Thompson played a massive part alongside the established Cliff Watson, Doug Laughton and Malcolm Reilly, to totally dominate the Australian pack. That form, and that dominance, was maintained in a sensational third Test decider in Sydney in which Great Britain scored five tries to one, but only managed to win 21-17 as a succession of penalties helped keep the Aussies in the game. It had been wonderful triumph for Frank Myler and his 1970 Lions.

(Above)
Glory day as British captain Frank Myler is carried aloft by Dave Chisnall, Chris Hesketh and Barry Seabourne after the Ashes were clinched in the 1970 third Test in Sydney.

(Above) Great Britain winger Alan Smith outpaces the Australian centre John McDonald in the 1970 second Test at the Sydney Cricket Ground - won by the Lions 28-7.

(Left)
The 1970 Lions.
Left to right: *(Back row)*: Reilly, Robinson, Smith, Price, Atkinson, Laughton, Thompson, Hesketh. *(Third row)*: Seabourne, Hepworth, Ward, Hardisty, Edwards, Flanagan, Millward. *(Second row)*: Chisnall, Irving, Sullivan, Fisher, Shoebottom, Hynes. *(Front row)*: Dutton, Hartley, Jack Harding (manager), Myler (captain), Johnny Whiteley (coach), Lowe and Watson.

The biggest star of the tour had been swashbuckling loose-forward Malcolm Reilly, despite a few off-field incidents which the Aussie press blew up in sensational style. With crowds of over 60,000 for both the Tests in Sydney, the tour was a massive financial success for the British Rugby League with each player receiving a record bonus of £790

TOUR RECORD

In Australia:
Played 17; Won 15; Lost 1; Drew 1.
Won Test series: 2-1.
In New Zealand:
Played 7; Won 7; Lost 0; Drew 0.
Won Test series: 3-0.
Tour totals:
Played 24; Won 22; Lost 1; Drew 1.
First game:
22nd May - at Darwin (N.T.)
Last game:
27th July - at Auckland.

TEST RESULTS

At Brisbane:
AUSTRALIA beat GB: 37-15.
At Sydney:
GB beat AUSTRALIA: 28-7.
At Sydney:
GB beat AUSTRALIA: 21-17.
At Auckland:
GB beat NEW ZEALAND: 19-15.
At Christchurch:
GB beat NEW ZEALAND: 23-9.
At Auckland:
GB beat NEW ZEALAND: 33-16.

(Above) Roger Millward, a star of the 1970 Ashes win, in the Second Test.

THE 1970 LIONS

John Atkinson (Leeds)	Terry Price (Bradford Northern)
Dave Chisnall (Leigh)	Malcolm Reilly (Castleford)
Ray Dutton (Widnes)	Dave Robinson (Wigan)
Derek Edwards (Castleford)	Barry Seabourne (Leeds)
Tony Fisher (Bradford North.)	Mick Shoebottom (Leeds)
Peter Flanagan (Hull K.R.)	Alan Smith (Leeds)
Alan Hardisty (Castleford)	Clive Sullivan (Hull)
Dennis Hartley (Castleford)	Jimmy Thompson (Featherstone)
Keith Hepworth (Castleford)	Johnny Ward (Salford)
Chris Hesketh (Salford)	Cliff Watson (St.Helens)
Syd Hynes (Leeds)	
Bob Irving (Oldham)	*Manager:*
Doug Laughton (Wigan)	Mr. Jack Harding (Leigh)
Phil Lowe (Hull K.R.)	*Coach:*
Roger Millward (Hull K.R.)	Johnny Whiteley (Hull)
Frank Myler (St.Helens)	

GREAT
BRITAIN
IN THE
1970s

Steve Nash -
an outstanding figure of
the decade for Britain in
the international arena.

(*Above*) Brian Lockwood, pictured before turning in a
man-of-the-match performance for Great Britain in the
1978 Second Test victory over Australia at Odsal.
Lockwood was one of the great talents of the decade
who missed out on more Test caps because he was in
such big demand by Australian clubs - but Brian was a
World Cup winner in 1972, and played in home Ashes
series of '73 and '78, before touring as a Lion in 1979.

The Great Britain team,
coached by Peter Fox and captained by
Roger Millward, before going on to beat Australia at
Odsal Stadium in the second Test of the 1978 Ashes series -
a match which has gone down in history as the 'Dad's Army' Test.

A trio of major figures in Great Britain colours
throughout the 'Seventies - *(above)* Phil Lowe
in action against Australia's Mick Cronin in
1978 - Lowe also played in the 1973 Ashes
series, was a World Cup winner in 1972 and a
member of the 1970 Lions touring team.
(Left, above) John Atkinson, the classic winger
who was an Ashes winner in 1970 and a World
Cup winner in 1972, who also toured with the
1974 Lions and played in the 1978 Ashes.
(Left, below) Big Jim Mills, who was selected
for every Lions tour down-under in the 1970s,
although he only made the 1974 and '79 trips.

LIONS ON TOUR 1974

(Above)
Lions captain Chris Hesketh discusses a decision with referee Don Lancashire in the first Test of the 1974 Ashes series, lost by Great Britain 12-6 at Lang Park, Brisbane.

Salford centre Chris Hesketh became the first Wigan born man to captain a Great Britain touring team when he lead the 1974 Lions down-under, along with Jim Challinor (St.Helens) as coach and Reg Parker (Blackpool Borough) the tour manager. And Hesketh's team were desperately unlucky not to come home with the Ashes from Australia, whilst they recovered from much adversity to win the Test series in New Zealand. The 1974 Lions were a side shorn of a host of top British stars who had been signed by Sydney clubs, including a whole pack of first choice international forwards who were forced to watch from the sidelines as their countrymen battled the Aussies for the Ashes. Great Britain were left kicking themselves after losing the first Test in Brisbane 12-6 in which the Australians scored the game's only try and the British missed numerous chances. When the Lions were decimated by injuries in the lead up to the vital second Test in Sydney, the Aussies became the hottest of favourites – but they reckoned without the bulldog spirit which saw Hesketh's team turn on a brilliant performance of skill mixed with sheer guts, and brought a 16-11 win on a day which had echoes of the legendary "Rorke's Drift" Test. With the half-back partnership of Ken Gill and Steve Nash turning on the style, Roger Millward helped the injury crisis by playing on the wing as the series was levelled. The deciding third Test was a thriller, which Britain led 16-12 at half-time, only to fall by four points to an Australian side inspired by the brilliance of skipper Graeme Langlands, playing his farewell Test.

With so many top players unavailable for the tour a new star was unearthed in the hooker/prop John Gray. Selected for the tour after just one season in Rugby League with Wigan, the former Coventry Rugby Union player showed plenty of courage and brilliant goal-kicking in the side-foot style which made big headlines in Australia. Such were the tourists' injury problems that the 1974 Lions were the first to have replacement players, as John Atkinson and John Bates were forced to return home and Maurice Richards and Bill Ramsey flew out to replace them. Gray finished as the tour's top points scorer with 111, whilst winger David Redfearn was the top try-scorer with 18.

(Above) John Gray, who shot to fame on the 1974 Lions tour, looks on as Australians Bobby Fulton and John Lang challenge for the ball in the opening moments of the second Test, won in superb style by Great Britain 16-11 at Sydney Cricket Ground.

(*Above*) The 1974 Lions pictured at Headingley. Left to right: (*Standing*): Ashcroft, Redfearn, Nicholas, Gray, Dyl, Atkinson, Dixon, Chisnall, Mills, Norton, John Bates, Willicombe, Rose, Clawson, Nicholls, Butler. (*Seated*): Alan Bates, Bevan, Eckersley, Charlton, Gill, Jim Challinor (coach), Hesketh (captain), Reg Parker (manager), Millward, Bridges, Nash and Watkins. (Before the team left for Australia Nicholas withdrew and was replaced by Jim Thompson).

After going so close in Australia, the Lions recovered from a first Test loss in New Zealand to win the series against the Kiwis. Injuries forced the coach Jim Challinor to turn out againt South Island at Greymouth. Hesketh was a fine captain who led from the front, and the financial success of the tour was assured for the British Rugby League thanks to the Lions' brilliant backs-to-the-wall win in the second Test in Sydney. That ensured a bumper 55,000-plus crowd for the decider and helped create a £93,282 profit for the British.

TOUR RECORD
In Australia:
Played 20; Won 15; Lost 5.
Lost Test series: 2-1.
In New Zealand:
Played 8; Won 6; Lost 2.
Won Test series: 2-1.
Tour totals:
Played 28; Won 21; Lost 7.
First game:
26th May - at Darwin (N.T.)
Last game:
13th August - at Auckland.

TEST RESULTS
At Brisbane:
AUSTRALIA beat GB: 12-6.
At Sydney:
GB beat AUSTRALIA: 16-11.
At Sydney:
AUSTRALIA beat GB: 22-18.
At Auckland:
NEW ZEALAND beat GB: 13-8.
At Christchurch:
GREAT BRITAIN beat NZ: 17-8.
At Auckland:
GREAT BRITAIN beat NZ: 20-0.

THE 1974 LIONS

Kevin Ashcroft (Warrington)
John Atkinson (Leeds)
Alan Bates (Dewsbury)
John Bates (Dewsbury)
John Bevan (Warrington)
Keith Bridges (Featherstone R.)
John Butler (Rochdale Hornets)
Paul Charlton (Salford)
Eric Chisnall (St.Helens)
Terry Clawson (Oldham)
Colin Dixon (Salford)
Les Dyl (Leeds)
David Eckersley (St.Helens)
Ken Gill (Salford)
John Gray (Wigan)
Chris Hesketh (Salford)
Jim Mills (Widnes)
Roger Millward (Hull K.R.)

Steve Nash (Featherstone Rovers)
George Nicholls (St.Helens)
Steve Norton (Castleford)
David Redfearn (Bradford N.)
Paul Rose (Hull K.R.)
Jimmy Thompson (Featherstone)
David Watkins (Salford)
David Willicombe (Wigan)
Replacements players:
Bill Ramsey (Bradford Northern)
(for John Bates)
Maurice Richards (Salford)
(for John Atkinson)

Manager:
Mr. Reg Parker (Blackpool Boro')
Coach:
Jim Challinor (St.Helens)

THE RED DEVILS

ALFORD v. Workington T.
SCENE
Vol. 3
No. 8
11.10.74
7p

'KING' DAVID ABDICATES (See page 10)
(Picture: Rugby Leaguer)

CHAMPIONS 1973/74

(Left) **John Butler, supported by John Knighton and Eric Prescott, on the attack for the Champions Salford in 1975-76.** *(Below)* **The captains - Chris Hesketh and David Watkins.**

GLAMOUR AND GLORY AT THE WILLOWS

The shining light through all of Rugby League's darkest times in the early '70s was Salford. With their ambitious Chairman, Brian Snape, at the helm, the Red Devils developed social facilities at The Willows which were the envy of other sporting clubs throughout the country. With that came Mr. Snape's search for a team to play exciting open rugby - the Salford style became a benchmark for Rugby League. Big stars like David Watkins, Colin Dixon, Chris Hesketh, Paul Charlton, Mike Coulman and Maurice Richards had already arrived in the late 1960s, and they continued to sign players throughout the '70s in the quest for more glamour and glory.

(*Above*) **Mike Coulman drives Salford forward against St.Helens in 1976, with John Knighton and Steve Nash in close support.**

SALFORD'S BIG SIGNINGS IN THE 'SEVENTIES

Here's a list of the Salford signings in the 'Seventies who cost £3,000 or more - there were several other good value recruits.

Player	Position	Date signed	From	Fee
Johnny Ward	*prop*	Jan.1970	Castleford	£6,000
Derek Clarke	*hooker*	Sept.1970	Swinton	£7,000
Bill Kirkbride	*back-row*	Jan.1971	Castleford	£6,000
Eric Prescott	*back-row*	Sept.1972	St.Helens	£13,500*
Peter Walker	*hooker*	Sept.1972	Bradford	£3,750
Barry Kear	*back-row*	Jan.1973	Featherstn.	£4,500
Keith Fielding	*wing*	May 1973	Moseley RU	£8,500
Paul Grimes	*prop*	Nov.1973	Leigh	£3,000
Gordon Graham	*centre*	Sept.1974	Sale RU	£3,000
Tom Brophy	*stand-off*	Nov.1974	Rochdale	£3,250
Jim Fiddler	*prop*	Jan.1975	Leigh	£10,000
John Butler	*stand-off*	Mar.1975	Rochdale	£7,000
Steve Nash	*scrum-half*	Aug.1975	Featherstone	£15,000*
Dean Raistrick	*hooker*	Dec.1975	Keighley	£5,000
John Mantle	*prop*	Aug.1976	St.Helens	£3,000
Bob Irving	*forward*	Nov.1977	Wigan	£6,750
Harold Henney	*back-row*	Jan.1978	Workington	£4,000
Ronnie Dootson	*back-row*	Dec.1978	Wigan	£4,500
David Stephenson	*centre*	Dec.1978	Fylde RU	£10,000
Graeme Johns	*full-back*	Dec.1978	Swinton	£8,000
Tony Gourley	*prop*	Jan.1979	Rochdale	£10,000
Ken Gill	*stand-off*	Aug.1979	Barrow	£12,000

* denotes Rugby League record transfer fee.
(Note: Ken Gill transferred from Salford to Widnes in Feb.1978, he later moved to Barrow and was re-sgined by Salford in Aug.1979.

(*Above*)
Friday nights under lights at The Willows brought a new excitement to Rugby League and was a big attraction for the sporting public around Manchester. It ensured the Red Devils had plenty of celebrity friends and admirers in the national press on Dean Street in the 1970s - as this supporting advert from three of the country's top selling tabloids for the Chris Hesketh and David Watkins Testimonial shows.

LIONS ON TOUR 1979

On the surface a tour record of 21 wins from a total of 27 matches, with five losses and one draw, does not look bad. It certainly would compare well to several previous Lions trips, but the 1979 Great Britain tour came to be regarded as an unprecedented disaster. The bottom line was that this British team became the first to lose an Ashes series 3-nil, and the result of their unimpressive performances against Australia ended up with this being the very first Lions tour in history to make a financial loss. Instead of the usual substantial profit from a Lions tour, in 1979 the British Rugby League suffered a loss of £31,590.

Captained by Doug Laughton, one of the stars of the 1970 Ashes win and a man who had been set to captain the 1974 Lions before he chose to take up an offer from an Australian club, and coached by Eric Ashton of St.Helens, a former successful Lions captain himself, the 1979 touring team used more players than ever before. They departed British shores with a squad of 30 players rather than the usual 26, and even had problems getting this side together to start the tour after the only wingers originally selected, Stuart Wright and John Bevan withdrew because of injuries and were replaced by Roy Mathias and David Barends. The South African Barends thus becoming the first non-Briton to become a Lion. Another original selection, Ken Kelly, broke his jaw two days before departure and was replaced by John Holmes; and there was more pre-tour controversy with the selection of prop Jim Mills, despite him being banned by the New Zealand Rugby League from playing in their country.

(Above)
Doug Laughton - captain of the 1979 Lions, but forced to leave the tour early because of an injury.

Once in Australia, the tour started in North Queensland and quickly ran into a succession of injury problems. The first Test in Brisbane attracted a crowd of only 23,051, the lowest for a Lions Test in Australia since 1910. Worse was to follow for the 1979 team. After a disastrous 35-nil thrashing in that first Test, injured players Jim Mills (thus diverting a future problem once the team got to New Zealand), Tommy Martyn and Roger Millward had to leave the tour, with John Burke, George Fairbairn and David Topliss being flown out to replace them. The original ommission of Fairbairn had been one of numerous selection blunders. Soon after, skipper Laughton and scrum-half Steve Nash also had their tours finished by injuries. From the debris of this patched up team, the man who stepped up to the plate to do his best to keep the tour on the rails was George Nicholls – he took over the captaincy of the team and moved up to the open-side prop position, showing tremendous courage to truly lead the Lions from the front. Under the captaincy of Nicholls, Great Britain put in a much better performance in the second Test in Sydney which, at one stage, looked like they might be able to square the

(Above)
George Nicholls captaining Great Britain for the first time in the second Test in 1979 at Sydney.

series. But the Aussies held on to win 24-16 and the Ashes were gone, to be followed by a poor display in being hammered 28-2 in the third Test.

To the credit of Nicholls and those players left standing, they rallied to win the series in New Zealand by playing determined football in muddy conditions in the first two Tests and also defying the strong challenge of Auckland in the last match of the tour, but the 1979 Lions returned home to

(Above) The 1979 Lions touring team pictured in England before their departure for Australia. Left to right: *(Back row):* Smith, Casey, Stone, Watkinson, Mumby, Kelly, Ward, Lockwood, Martyn, Adams, Woods, Glynn. *(Middle row):* Mills, Wright, Norton, Nicholls, Mathias, James, Grayshon, Evans, Hogan, Skerrett, Joyner. *(Front row):* Eric Ashton (coach), Nash, Millward, Harry Womersley (manager), Laughton (captain), Dick Gemmell (manager), Stephens, Redfearn, Ronnie Barritt (physiotherapist). (Before the team left for Australia both Ken Kelly and Stuart Wright withdrew because of injuries, and were replaced by John Holmes and David Barends respectively).

much criticism about lack of discipline and lack of fitness, which prompted an investigation by the Rugby League Council. Among the recommendations made were that future tour selections should be made only two or three weeks before the tour, and that those players selected should have independent medical checks on their fitness before departure, with any man not being 100% fit ruled out. It was quite a wake up call for British Rugby League.

(Above) David Barends in 1979, as the first non Briton to become a British Lion.

TOUR RECORD

In Australia:
Played 18; Won 13; Lost 4; Drew 1.
Lost Test series: 3-0.

In New Zealand:
Played 9; Won 8; Lost 1; Drew 0.
Won Test series: 2-1.

Tour totals:
Played 27; Won 21; Lost 5; Drew 1.
First game:
25th May - at Mackay (North Qld.)
Last game:
13th August - At Auckland.

TEST RESULTS

At Brisbane:
AUSTRALIA beat GB: 35-0.
At Sydney:
AUSTRALIA beat GB: 24-16.
At Sydney:
AUSTRALIA beat GB: 28-2.
At Auckland:
GB beat NEW ZEALAND: 16-8.
At Christchurch:
GB beat NEW ZEALAND: 22-7.
At Auckland:
NEW ZEALAND beat GB: 18-11.

THE 1979 LIONS

Mick Adams (Widnes)
David Barends (Bradford N.)
Len Casey (Bradford N.)
Steve Evans (Featherstone R.)
Peter Glynn (St.Helens)
Jeff Grayshon (Bradford N.)
Phil Hogan (Hull K.R.)
John Holmes (Leeds)
Eric Hughes (Widnes)
Mel James (St.Helens)
John Joyner (Castleford)
Doug Laughton (Widnes)
Graham Liptrot (St.Helens)
Brian Lockwood (Hull K.R.)
Tommy Martyn (Warrington)
Roy Mathias (St.Helens)
Jim Mills (Widnes)
Keith Mumby (Bradford N.)
Steve Nash (Salford)
George Nicholls (St.Helens)
Steve Norton (Hull)

Alan Redfearn (Bradford N.)
Trevor Skerrett (Wakefield T.)
Mike Smith (Hull K.R.)
Gary Stephens (Castleford)
Richard 'Charlie' Stone (Hull)
David Ward (Leeds)
David Watkinson (Hull K.R.)
John Woods (Leigh)
Replacement players:
George Fairbairn (Wigan)
(for Tommy Martyn)
John Burke (Wakefield Trinity)
(for Jim Mills)
David Topliss (Wakefield Trinity)
(for Roger Millward)

Managers:
Mr. Harry Womersley (Bradford)
Mr. Dick Gemmell (Hull)
Coach:
Eric Ashton MBE (St.Helens)

KANGAROOS ON TOUR

1973

(Right)
The 1973 Kangaroo touring team were based during their stay in England at the George Hotel in Huddersfield, famous for being the birthplace of the game. Here the Australians wave hello for the cameraman on arrival at the George Hotel. Bobby Fulton is the only one bracing himself for the English weather by wearing a coat.

(Right)
Dewsbury, as the reigning Champions of the Rugby League, met the 1973 Aussie touring team - here scrum-half Alan Bates is tackled as the Kangaroos won 17-3.

THE 1973 KANGAROOS IN BRITAIN

September		Result		Att.
Sun. 30	Salford	Won	15-12	11,064
October				
Wed. 3	Wakefield T.	Won	13-9	5,863
Sun. 7	Dewsbury	Won	17-3	5,685
Wed. 10	Castleford	Won	18-10	2,419
Sun. 14	Widnes	Won	25-10	5,185
Fri. 19	Oldham	Won	44-10	2,895
Wed. 24	Cumbria	Won	28-2	3,666
Sun. 28	Bradford N.	Won	50-14	5,667
November				
Sat. 3	**GT. BRITAIN (1)**	**Lost**	**12-21**	**9,874**
Wed. 7	Hull K.R.	Won	25-9	5,150
Sat. 10	Huddersfield	Won	32-2	1,333
Sun. 11	Leigh	Won	31-4	2,607
Tue. 13	St. Helens	Lost	7-11	10,013
Sun. 18	Featherstone	Won	18-13	5,659
Sat. 24	**GT. BRITAIN (2)**	**Won**	**14-6**	**16,674**
December				
Sat. 1	**GT. BRITAIN (3)**	**Won**	**15-5**	**10,019**

The first full Kangaroo tour for six years arrived in 1973 with the Australians knowing that since their previous tour in 1967 they had relinquished to Great Britain both the Ashes in 1970 and the World Cup in 1972. That, and the fact that they faced the adversity of having to play without their injured captain Graeme Langlands, and vice-captain Bob McCarthy, meant their joy at winning an Ashes-deciding third Test on a freezing day at Warrington was overwhelming – and enough to make them forget all the problems encountered on a difficult tour marred by poor attendances. The inevitable shortfall in gate receipts meant the 1973 Kangaroos made a loss rather than a profit, as they toured at a time when the British game was at its lowest ebb. The game's struggle for crowds was made worse for the Australians by a poorly thought out itinerary which saw them miss matches against big clubs like Leeds, Wigan and Warrington. The nadir came in a Saturday fixture at Huddersfield which drew only 1,333 spectators to a dilapidated Fartown. The tour manager Charlie

Gibson was critical of the British Rugby League's planning, and the fact that live television was allowed to hit attendances so badly. However, the Aussies were thankful for broadcasting fees in excess of £5,000 for each of the three Tests which helped boost their miserly receipts. It was the Australians' insistence that a Test match be played in London (as had been the case on the previous two Kangaroo tours) which ensured they did not get to play at Wigan's Central Park – and it backfired on the Aussies as a crowd of only 9,875 were dotted around the empty spaces of Wembley Stadium as they were comprehensively beaten by Great Britain in the first Test.

Captained by Graeme Langlands, it was inevitable that this 1973 team would be known as "Chang's gang," and their skipper ran into trouble when he broke his hand against Leigh, opening the way for the 19-year-old full-back Graeme Eadie to make his Test debut in the crucial second rubber at Headingley. A close win there created a winner-takes-all showdown in the third Test on a Wilderspool pitch which was frozen hard, where the Australians played spectacularly to run in five tries, including two barnstorming efforts by second-rower Ken Maddison. The Ashes were reclaimed by Beetson, Fulton, O'Reilly and co.

THE RUGBY FOOTBALL LEAGUE
TEST MATCH

GREAT BRITAIN
v
AUSTRALIA
WEMBLEY STADIUM

Saturday, 3rd November 1973 . . . Kick-off 3 pm

Official programme . . . 10 pence

(Above) Programme
for the 1973 First Test
at Wembley Stadium.

TOUR RECORD
First game: 30th September 1973, at Salford.
Last game: 16th December 1973, at Toulouse.
In Britain:
Played 16; Won 14; Lost 2; Drew 0.
Won Test series: 2-1.
In France:
Played 3; Won 3; Lost 0; Drew 0.
Won Test series: 2-0.

TEST RESULTS
G.B. beat AUSTRALIA 21-12 (*at Wembley*)
AUSTRALIA beat G.B. 14-6 (*at Headingley*)
AUSTRALIA beat G.B. 15-5 (*at Warrington*)
AUSTRALIA beat FRANCE 21-9 (*at Perpignan*)
AUSTRALIA beat FRANCE 14-3 (*at Toulouse*)

(*Above*) **Bob Fulton gets his pass away for the Australians in their 24-12 win over France 'B' at Bordeaux - the only midweek fixture in France on the 1973 Kangaroo tour.**

KANGAROOS ON TOUR

1978

(Right)
Coach Frank Stanton and captain Bobby Fulton lead the 1978 Kangaroos down the Odsal steps and onto the pitch ready to do battle in the Second Test. You can see groups of Australian supporters in the grandstand, but they were to leave Odsal Stadium disappointed as Fulton's team went on to lose this Test to Great Britain's so-called "Dad's Army" side.

The 1978 Ashes Series was the first to be sponsored in Great Britain, as the Widnes based company Forward Chemicals injected £17,500 to be associated with the series.

The 1978 Kangaroos went home from Europe with only two Test wins and three Test losses, but their tour was acclaimed as an undoubted success with the primary target – retention of the Ashes – safely achieved. More so, the Australians of 1978 laid the foundations for what was to follow with the "Invincibles" of the 'eighties, living in style at the Dragonara Hotel in Leeds and showing signs of a new level of athleticism and professionalism that would bring them a decade of domination over the British. Captained by Bob Fulton, making his second Kangaroo tour, the 1978 Aussies found a totally revitalised Rugby League scene in England compared to the dark days of their 1973 tour, and this showed in the vastly increased attendances who watched them play, leading to a healthy profit for the Australians with each of their 28 players picking up a bonus of $1,250. Coach Frank Stanton broke new ground in preparation, whereas most previous Kangaroo touring teams had relied on the captain to also coach the side.

The 1978 tour got off to gentle start at Blackpool, a breeze against Cumbria at Barrow, and broke new ground with a game against the British Under-24s at Hull K.R.'s Craven Park. The Australians also played Wales in Swansea, following up their clash there in the 1975 World Championship, and

THE 1978 KANGAROOS IN BRITAIN

September		Result		Att.
Sat. 30	Blackpool B.	Won	39-1	2,700
October				
Sun. 1	Cumbria	Won	47-4	5,964
Wed. 4	Gt. Britain U-24s	Won	30-8	6,418
Sun. 8	Bradford N.	Won	21-11	15,755
Wed. 11	Warrington	Lost	12-15	10,143
Sun. 15	Wales	Won	8-3	4,250
Tue. 17	Leeds	Won	25-19	9,781
Sun. 21	**GT. BRITAIN (1)**	**Won**	**15-9**	**17,644**
Wed 25	Widnes	Lost	10-11	12,232
Sun. 29	Hull	Won	34-2	10,723
November				
Wed. 1	Salford	Won	14-2	6,115
Sun . 5	**GT. BRITAIN (2)**	**Lost**	**14-18**	**26,447**
Wed. 8	Wigan	Won	28-2	10,645
Sun. 12	St. Helens	Won	26-4	16,342
Tue. 14	York	Won	29-2	5,155
Sat . 18	GT. BRITAIN (3)	Won	23-6	29,627

(Left)
The 1978 tour started at Blackpool, and although the Aussies won comfortably, they did experience a few moments of being bamboozled by the veteran scrum-half Bak Diabira - seen here slipping a switch pass to prop Jimmy Hamilton. Other Blackpool Borough players in the back-ground are Norman Turley, Derek Watts and winger Graham Pitchforth

had a series of rugged and exciting clashes against leading clubs. The Aussies had plenty of complaints about rough play and referees – notably in both their defeats to club sides, Warrington and Widnes, where the tourists scored more tries than the opposition but lost after a flood of penalties brought victory on goal-kicks for the home teams. But, as always, the real business came in the Test series and Fulton's men, with his half-back partner Tom Raudonikis always a key and controver-sial figure, faced a tough battle. The first Test at Wigan was on a knife edge and could have gone either way before Australia edged home late in the game; that led to a showdown at Odsal - it was the first Ashes Test to be played on a Sunday and drew the biggest crowd for an international game in Britain since the 1963 tour. Coached by Peter Fox and with several recalled vet-erans which gave rise to their team being nicknamed "Dad's Army," Great Britain squared the series, leading to a deciding third Test which rapidly sold out Headingley's capacity of just short of 30,000. That expectant crowd wit-nessed a stunning first half by the Australians which signalled a real chang-ing of the guard in the world of Rugby League. The Kangaroos retained the Ashes with plenty to spare, but they were brought down to earth when they moved on to France for the second leg of their tour – against a tough and deter-mined French team, Australia lost both Tests. To rub salt in the wounds of the Kangaroos' pride, they also lost a third match in France against the French Under-24s at Albi, when Fulton's team lost all their discipline in the face of a 33-2 penalty count and were beaten 20-5 (the French side's points coming from ten penalty goals.)

(Above)
Australian captain Bob Fulton, back in the town of his birth, exchanges pennants with the Warrington skipper Billy Benyon before a fiery match at Wilderspool which saw the Kangaroos defeated 15-12. The Aussies also went on to lose against Widnes 11-10, but their biggest shocks came in France where loose-forward Michel Maique captained the French to a 2-nil Test series victory, a repeat of the 1967 Kangaroos defeat in France after also winning the Ashes in England.

TOUR RECORD

First game: 30th September 1978, at Blackpool.
Last game: 10th December 1978, at Toulouse.
In Britain:
Played 16; Won 13; Lost 3; Drew 0.
Won Test series: 2-1.
In France:
Played 6; Won 3; Lost 3; Drew 0.
Lost Test series: 2-0.

TEST RESULTS

AUSTRALIA beat G.B. 15-9 *(at Wigan)*
G.B. beat AUSTRALIA 18-14 *(at Bradford)*
AUSTRALIA beat G.B. 23-6 *(at Headingley)*
FRANCE beat AUSTRALIA 13-10 *(at Carcassonne)*
FRANCE beat AUSTRALIA 11-10 *(at Toulouse)*

THE KIWIS TOUR 1971

(Above)
The 1971 Kiwis perform their haka before clinching the Test series against Great Britain at Castleford. Only 3,925 spectators were at Wheldon Road to see New Zealand win this second Test 17-14 in a contest of high drama.

New Zealand Rugby League had never enjoyed a year like 1971, as the amateur Kiwis ruled the world after walloping Australia 24-3 in Auckland, then winning Test series against both Great Britain and France on their own soil. Their triumph in Britain was a first series win in the mother country since the original "All Golds" touring team of 1908. Winning the first two Tests against the British enabled the 1971 Kiwi touring team to earn a revered place in Rugby League history, with special acclaim for their captain Roy Christian, and throughout Britain and France this New Zealand side were popular visitors for their crisp attacking football and good sportsmanship. They set out on the tour hardly expecting such glory, as a team of amateurs, and after a disappointing show in the 1970 World Cup, many critics thought they would not be able to match it against the best professional clubs in England to say nothing of the British and French international teams. An overall tour record in England of losing ten of their twenty fixtures might concur with such predictions, but among their ten victories were two vital ones in the first two Tests.

The 1971 Kiwis had the misfortune of coming to England when Rugby League was struggling to maintain its public appeal. Attendance figures for the three Tests hit rock bottom, and it was visibly shocking for the game's officials when only 3,764 turned up at Salford for the first Test. After-match inquests claimed the Salford public were in the habit of watching Rugby League on Friday nights, and would not attend on a Saturday afternoon, and it was ironic that whilst all three Test crowds were pitifully small, the games were watched by several million viewers live on BBC Television. Another shock for British officials was New Zealand's 18-13 victory in that first Test.

THE 1971 KIWIS IN BRITAIN

September		Result		Att.
Sat. 4	Rochdale H.	Won	23-8	2,374
Mon. 6	St. Helens	Lost	8-18	8,169
Wed. 8	Hull K.R.	Lost	10-12	5,746
Sun. 12	Widnes	Won	18-15	5,787
Wed. 15	Castleford	Lost	8-25	5,889
Sat. 18	Warrington	Lost	2-13	6,295
Sat. 25	**GT. BRITAIN (1)**	**Won**	**18-13**	**3,764**
Thu. 30	Barrow	Won	25-15	4,839
October				
Sat. 2	Whitehaven	Won	21-8	3,105
Fri. 8	Swinton	Lost	15-26	3,280
Sun. 10	Wigan	Won	24-10	12,187
Sat. 16	**GT. BRITAIN (2)**	**Won**	**17-14**	**3,925**
Sun. 17	Huddersfield	Lost	10-11	3,495
Wed 20	Leigh	Lost	5-10	4,012
Fri. 22	Salford	Lost	30-31	7,127
Sun. 24	Wakefield T.	Won	23-12	5,367
Wed. 27	Oldham	Won	24-13	2,172
Sat. 30	Bradford N.	Won	30-23	6,362
Sun. 31	York	Lost	5-11	2,803
November				
Sat. 6	**GT. BRITAIN (3)**	**Lost**	**3-12**	**5,479**

(*Above*) **Key moments in the second Test against the Kiwis in 1971 at Wheldon Road, Castleford, as Great Britain twice got over the line in the second half but both times dropped the ball when hit by New Zealand tacklers. The unfortunate British players were (*left*) Billy Benyon and (*right*) Joe Walsh.**

With Roy Christian an inspiring captain the Kiwis came back from an early deficit to win, with a magical moment being provided by their stand-off Dennis Williams, on the day after his 18th birthday, when he swooped for a brilliant solo try with his first touch of the ball in Test match rugby.

New Zealand clinched the series with a controversial 17-14 win in the second Test at Castleford. Among the stars of the tour were mighty prop Henry Tatana and the dynamic winger Phil Orchard, and there was some dispute over whether Orchard had stepped in touch on the way to his winning try. It was a close shave, and even closer for the Kiwis as twice Great Britain got over the line in the closing stages, but dropped the ball in the act of scoring. Another star was scrum-half Ken Stirling, and New Zealand were angry when he was forced to leave the field after a high tackle by Alex Murphy, recalled to the British side for what proved to be his last Test appearance. Unprecedented success followed for the 1971 Kiwis in France, where they went undefeated in six games, including a three Test series in which they won the first two in brilliant style then drew the third.

Henry Tatana set to score in the second Test as G.B.'s Alex Murphy and Mick Stephenson are beaten.

TOUR RECORD

First game: 4th September 1971, at Rochdale.
Last game: 28th November 1971, at Toulouse.
In Britain:
Played 20; Won 10; Lost 10; Drew 0.
Won Test series: 2-1.
In France:
Played 6; Won 5; Drew 1; Lost 0.
Won Test series: 2-0, plus 1 draw.

TEST RESULTS

NEW ZEALAND beat G.B. 18-13 (*at Salford*)
NEW ZEALAND beat G.B. 17-14 (*at Castleford*)
G.B. beat NEW ZEALAND 12-1 (*at Headingley*)
N. ZEALAND beat FRANCE 27-11 (*at Perpignan*)
N.ZEALAND beat FRANCE 24-2 (*at Carcassonne*)
N.ZEALAND & FRANCE drew 3-3 (*at Toulouse*)

(*Above*) **The Kiwis' finest display of the 1971 tour came in their 24-2 second Test win over France at Carcassonne. Here New Zealand's John Whittaker attacks with Phil Orchard in support, as the 18-year-old French debutant Bernard Guilhem gives chase.**

Note: The 1971 Kiwis also played two friendlies in London versus Southern Amateur X111s, on 29th and 30th August, before travelling north to begin their tour in earnest. New Zealand won 67-6 and 66-nil, but these games are not included in official tour records.

GREAT BRITAIN'S OTHER TEST MATCHES

(Right) French centre Jacques Gruppi makes the break that created a try for his winger Jean-Marie Bonal, the former Rugby Union cap, as France won 16-8 at Toulouse in 1971. The British forwards giving chase in the background are David Jeanes, in his Test debut, and John Mantle.

(Above) Bill Ashurst about to score one of his two tries as Great Britain thrashed France 45-10 at Odsal in 1972. In support are Nicholls and Stephenson.

1970-71
7th February 1971 - at Le Stadium Municipal, Toulouse.
FRANCE beat GREAT BRITAIN 16-8. *Att. 14,960.*
17th March 1971 - at Knowsley Road, St.Helens.
GREAT BRITAIN beat FRANCE 24-2. *Att. 7,783.*
1971-72
6th February 1972 - at Le Stadium Municipal, Toulouse.
GREAT BRITAIN beat FRANCE 10-9. *Att. 11,508.*
12th March 1972 - at Odsal Stadium, Bradford.
GREAT BRITAIN beat FRANCE 45-10. *Att. 7,313.*
1973-74
20th January 1974 - at Stade Municipal, Grenoble.
GREAT BRITAIN beat FRANCE 24-5. *Att. 4,100.*
17th February 1974 - at Central Park, Wigan.
GREAT BRITAIN beat FRANCE 29-0. *Att. 9,108.*

In addition to their crowded fixture list of Tests against Australia and New Zealand, along with the four World Cups staged in the 'Seventies, Great Britain also played three seasons of home and away Tests with France, before the re-birth of the Welsh team in 1975 meant a revival of the European Championship. Less than a year after winning the Ashes, Britain's team were well beaten in Toulouse in 1971, but thereafter they dominated France.

Great Britain's record during the 'Seventies could have been very different were it not for controversial refereeing decisions in three crucial events – all, ironically, by British officials. The first came in the 1973 Ashes, with Great Britain already one up in the series and the second Test at Headingley in the balance, referee Billy Thompson sent off Brian Lockwood for a "high tackle" on Bobby Fulton. Even Fulton expressed his surprise that Lockwood was dismissed – leaving Britain to play a man short for almost all the second-half. The second crucial decision, again involving Mr. Thompson, was in the 1977 World Cup Final in Sydney, when he stopped play to give a penalty to Great Britain for obstruction just as winger Stuart Wright was striding clear to go under the posts. Britain went on to lose that match by just one point. The third refereeing body-blow was in the 1978 Ashes first Test at Wigan, when official Ron Campbell sent off scrum-half Steve Nash who was only trying to defend himself from assault by Tom Raudonikis. In that 1978 Test, Nash was Britain's key player, and having him off the field changed the game.

THE WORLD CUPS

1970

(Above) French captain Jean-Pierre Clar passes from a scrum in his team's victory over Australia at Odsal.
(Above, right) Great Britain match winner, full-back Ray Dutton in possession against France at Castleford.

Great Britain entered the 1970 World Cup as hot favourites to regain the honour they had last won on their own soil ten years earlier. Playing at home, and just a few months after outclassing Australia in Sydney to win the Ashes, the British side captained by Frank Myler expected to have the measure of the Aussies. All seemed to be going to plan as Great Britain won their way through to the World Cup Final undefeated, including an 11-4 victory over Australia at Headingley – but it all went wrong when the two sides met again two weeks later at the same venue. Some British players seemed more interested in bashing the Ashes rather than playing the constructive rugby which had won the Ashes. Crucially, Great Britain were missing the injured Roger Millward from the Ashes team. Australia, captained by Ron Coote, won the World Cup Final 12-7, and the game suffered some hysterical headlines in the media after punches were exchanged at the end.

Australia were lucky to even be in the World Cup Final in 1970, as France were left kicking themselves for losing by one point against New Zealand despite scoring three tries to two. That game, played at the Boulevard in Hull, featured a 100-metre try by the French winger Serge Marsolan. The French had a good team in 1970, as they went on to prove by beating Australia at Odsal and going toe to toe with Great Britain in the rain at Castleford, where the British needed three penalities by full-back Ray Dutton to give them their 6-nil victory. With Great Britain unbeaten with three wins from three, all the other nations finished equal with one win and two defeats apiece, leaving Australia to pip France for a place in the final on points scoring difference.

The 1970 World Cup was the first to be sponsored, by a company called V. & G. Insurance, who provided a new, one-off, trophy. The Aussies had brought the original World Cup with them and it was stolen from their hotel in Bradford – never to be seen again for almost 25 years.

(Above)
Malcolm Reilly in the 1970 World Cup Final.

1970 WORLD CUP RESULTS

21st October - at Central Park, Wigan
AUSTRALIA beat NEW ZEALAND 47-11.
24th October - at Headingley, Leeds
GREAT BRITAIN beat AUSTRALIA 11-4.
25th October - at the Boulevard, Hull
NEW ZEALAND beat FRANCE 16-15.
28th October - at Wheldon Road, Castleford
GREAT BRITAIN beat FRANCE 6-0.
31st October - at Station Road, Swinton
GT.BRITAIN beat NEW ZEALAND 27-17.
1st November - at Odsal Stadium, Bradford
FRANCE beat AUSTRALIA 17-15.
The Final - 7th November - at Headingley, Leeds
AUSTRALIA beat GREAT BRITAIN 12-7.

THE WORLD CUPS

1972

The World Cup of 1972 will always be remembered as one of British Rugby League's greatest triumphs, with many comparisons to Great Britain's victory in the inaugural World Cup tournament in 1954. The fact that both were attained in France made for obvious similarities, and also that the British were underdogs again - in 1972 against a powerful Australian team. And just as Dave Valentine had been in 1954, the British team of '72 discovered a captain in Clive Sullivan who proved to be an inspirational leader.

Great Britain qualified for the 1972 World Cup Final with a 100% record, the key to their triumph coming in the opening match against Australia in Perpignan. The Aussies were unbackable favourites, but the British produced some wonderful attacking play in a rip-roaring game in front of a Catalan crowd clearly favouring the underdogs, to emerge 27-21 winners. They followed that with a hard fought midweek win over France in Grenoble where second-rower Phil Lowe proved an unstoppable force for the dogged French defenders, and then

(Above)
Great Britain's moment of triumph on 11th November, 1972, as captain Clive Sullivan takes the World Cup on a lap of honour at the Stade Gerland in Lyon. Joining Clive in the picture are Mick Stephenson, Chris Hesketh, Steve Nash (wearing an Aussie jersey), and Phil Lowe. A 10-all draw with Australia had enabled the British to win the World Cup.

a romp against the Kiwis in the pleasant surroundings of Pau in southwest France, the 53-19 scoreline setting new records, notably a 26-point haul for the Leeds teenager John Holmes.

The British team came home during the week in the build up to the final before returning to France to meet the Australians again at Lyon. An epic encounter was played in an eerie atmosphere with a tiny crowd of only 4,231 scattered around the huge *Stade Gerland*. The highlight was a sensational try by skipper Clive Sullivan which has gone down in the folkore of the game – Clive scooping up a loose-ball near his own line and sprinting 90 metres down the touchline to score. The Australians were denied what would have been a brilliant try by their captain, Graeme Langlands, who was controversially ruled offside after diving to take a kick by scrum-half Dennis Ward. When the match finished with the scores locked at 10-all, extra time was played without any further score, leaving Great Britain winners as the team with the best record in the qualifying games.

The 1972 World Cup was a major undertaking for the French Rugby League's new president Rene Mauries – eager to pursue a policy of expansion, an original itinerary which included a game in the stronghold of Carcassonne

(*Above*) **Australia's mighty centre-threequarter Mark Harris charges through the French defence in the 1972 World Cup match at Toulouse which the Aussies won 31-9, with Harris scoring two of their seven tries.**

and staging the final in Toulouse, gave way to flying the flag in venues like Pau, Grenoble, Paris and the final in Lyon. It backfired when it came to drawing spectators live in the stadiums, but enabled the French to attract substantial television fees and sponsorship which produced a profit of £68,000 for the four competing nations to share. British fans were able to enjoy live television coverage of the games on the BBC, with Eddie Waring producing one of his great moments of commentary as Clive Sullivan headed for his famous try, whilst live radio commentary was by Don Mosey. The victorious Great Britain team coach was Jim Challinor.

(*Above*) **Action from the 1972 World Cup Final, as Bob O'Reilly shapes to pass with the British cover closing in, lead by John Walsh, Terry Clawson, Mick Stephenson and Phil Lowe.**

The 1972 World Cup Final
GREAT BRITAIN 10, AUSTRALIA 10.
(*After extra-time. Score after 80 minutes was 10-10*).
Great Britain: Tries: Sullivan, Stephenson.
Goals: Clawson (2).
Australia: Tries: O'Neill, Beetson. Goals: Branighan (2).
GREAT BRITAIN: Paul Charlton (Salford); Clive Sullivan (Hull) capt., Chris Hesketh (Salford), John Walsh (St.Helens), John Atkinson (Leeds); John Holmes (Leeds), Steve Nash (Featherstone); Terry Clawson (Leeds), Mick Stephenson (Dewsbury), David Jeanes (Leeds), Phil Lowe (Hull K.R.), Brian Lockwood (Castleford), George Nicholls (Widnes).
Subs.: Dennis O'Neill (Widnes) *did not play*, Bob Irving (Oldham) for Jeanes.
AUSTRALIA: Graeme Langlands (capt.); John Grant, Mark Harris, Geoff Starling, Ray Branighan; Bob Fulton, Dennis Ward; John O'Neill, Elwyn Walters, Bob O'Reilly, Arthur Beetson, Gary Stevens, Gary Sullivan.
Subs.: Stephen Knight, Fred Jones (*neither played*).
Referee: Mr. Georges Jameau (France).

1972 WORLD CUP RESULTS
28th October- at Stade Velodrome, Marseille
FRANCE beat NEW ZEALAND 20-9.
29th October- at Stade Gilbert Brutus, Perpignan
GT.BRITAIN. beat AUSTRALIA 27-21.
1st November - at Stade Municipal, Grenoble
GT.BRITAIN beat FRANCE 13-4.
1st November - at Parc des Princes, Paris
AUSTRALIA beat NEW ZEALAND 9-5.
4th November - at Stade du Hameau, Pau
GT. BRITAIN beat NEW ZEALAND 53-19.
5th November - at Le Stadium Municipal, Toulouse
AUSTRALIA beat FRANCE 31-9.
The Final - 11th November - at Stade Gerland, Lyon
GT.BRITAIN & AUSTRALIA drew 10-10.
(After extra-time - Great Britain won the World Cup as they had most points from the qualifying games and had beaten Australia already in the tournament.)

THE WORLD CUPS

1975

O f all the crazy things Rugby League saw during the 1970s, the World Championship of 1975 took some beating. Sandwiched in between the World Cups of 1972 and '77, the 1975 competition stretched from March to November and was played across five different countries, only to end up with no climax. There was no *grand finale* as the winners were declared on the basis of who finished top of the league table, and fate had it that Australia were that team despite the fact

(*Above*) **Australia unveiled a new star when they came to Europe in 1975 in the shape of teenage winger Ian Schubert. He had toured three years earlier with the Australian Schoolboys team, and was an easy to recognise figure with his mane of blonde hair. In this picture Schubert is seen diving over for one of his hat-trick of tries for Australia in the match against England at Wigan. Unable to prevent the touchdown are full-back George Fairbairn and winger David Redfearn. On this occasion it could not stop England winning 16-13, but Schubert's star quality was emphasised when he also scored a hat-trick against Wales. (*Right*) England forward Phil Jackson seems to be battling the referee Harry Hunt as well as the French defence in the match at Headingley in March 1975.**

they could not beat England. With hindsight, it was a lesson in how *not* organise a World Championship, and the public voted with their feet with England's home games attracting very disappointing attendances. Their top crowd was the 10,842 for the match against France at Headingley, with embarrassingly low figures of 5,937 and 9,393 drawn for the games versus New Zealand and Australia at Bradford and Wigan respectively.

The novelty of the 1975 World Championship was that Wales competed as an independent team, leaving England to do battle rather than Great Britain. Ironically it was the Welsh who denied England the world title, in a match bizarrely staged in Brisbane, Australia, Wales beat England 12-7 in a brawling affair which left the English bruised and battered. England then dropped a point against New Zealand in Auckland before showing what a

WORLD CHAMPIONSHIP TABLE

	P	W	L	D	Pts.	For	Ag.
Australia	8	6	1	1	13	198	69
England	8	5	2	1	12	167	84
Wales	8	3	0	5	6	110	130
New Zealand	8	2	2	4	6	121	149
France	8	1	1	6	3	40	204

(Left)
Two of the game's all-time greats were rival captains in the 1975 World Championship, and in this action from England's win over Australia at Wigan, it's Roger Millward who gets ahead of Arthur Beetson. Millward's team were unbeaten against the Aussies, but Beetson still got to pick up the World Championship trophy after his team topped the table by one point from England.

The English coach in the 1975 World Championship was Alex Murphy, with Bill Oxley as team manager, and Alex did not let anybody forget that the Aussies could not beat his team. It was ironic that it was Wales who proved to the reason why England did not win the world title.

good team they really were by securing a second draw with Australia in Sydney. England's good form continued when they returned home for the second stage of the tournament in the autumn of 1975, as they achieved a record win on French soil, plus solid home wins over Wales, New Zealand and Australia. The game with the Aussies at Central Park was a thriller, and the key to England's success was the creative talents of their half-backs where they had Ken Gill, Steve Nash and skipper Roger Millward all vying for a place. David Watkins captained the Welsh team who made their first ever overseas tour to the southern hemisphere to take part.

1975 WORLD CHAMPIONSHIP RESULTS

First Section

2nd March - at Le Stadium Municipal, Toulouse.
FRANCE beat WALES 14-7.
16th March - at Headingley, Leeds
ENGLAND beat FRANCE 20-2.
1st June - at Lang Park, Brisbane
ASUTRALIA beat NEW ZEALAND 36-8.
10th June - at Lang Park, Brisbane
WALES beat ENGLAND 12-7.
14th June - at Sydney Cricket Ground
AUSTRALIA beat WALES 30-13.
15th June - at the Christchurch Show Grounds
NEW ZEALAND beat FRANCE 27-0.
21st June - at Carlaw Park, Auckland
NEW ZEALAND & ENGLAND drew 17-17.
22nd June - at Lang Park, Brisbane
AUSTRALIA beat FRANCE 26-6.
28th June - at Sydney Cricket Ground
AUSTRALIA & ENGLAND drew 10-10.
28th June - at Carlaw Park, Auckland
NEW ZEALAND beat WALES 13-8.

Second Section

20th September - at Wilderspool, Warrington
ENGLAND beat WALES 22-16.
27th September - at Carlaw Park, Auckland
AUSTRALIA beat NEW ZEALAND 24-8.
11th October - at Stade Municipal, Bordeaux
ENGLAND beat FRANCE 48-2.
17th October - at Stade Velodrome, Marseille
FRANCE & NEW ZEALAND drew 12-12.
19th October - at St.Helen's, Swansea
AUSTRALIA beat WALES 18-6.
25th October - at Odsal Stadium, Bradford
ENGLAND beat NEW ZEALAND 27-12.
26th October - at Stade Gilbert Brutus, Perpignan
AUSTRALIA beat FRANCE 41-2.
1st November - at Central Park, Wigan
ENGLAND beat AUSTRALIA 16-13.
2nd November - at St.Helen's, Swansea
WALES beat NEW ZEALAND 25-14.
6th November - at The Willows, Salford
WALES beat FRANCE 23-2.

The World Cups

One of Great Britain's bravest World Cup efforts came in 1977 as a team shorn of so many established international players went within a whisker of beating Australia on their own soil to claim the trophy. The British side had a new look about it as it set out for the first leg of the tournament in New Zealand with some trepidation – after all, England had finished last in the recent European Championship to a rampant French side, and they had only two forwards with previous experience of playing Test football down-under. Those two, Jimmy Thompson and George Nicholls, proved to be the inspirational rocks driving forward a pack with new stars Steve Pitchford, Eddie Bowman and Phil Hogan.

With a rookie coach in David Watkins, the wily manager Reg Parker knew his team needed to draw on the experience of men like captain Roger Millward and Steve Nash, who had toured before and knew all about playing in Australia and New Zealand. Great Britain got off to a perfect start with a convincing 23-4 win over France in sticky conditions in Auckland – full-back George Fairbairn's excellent goal-kicking from the Carlaw Park mud provided 14 points and there was a brilliant debut by the young Barrow loose-forward Phil Hogan. The British team clinched their place in the World Cup Final even before they got to Australia, by outclassing New Zealand 30-12 in Christchurch in their second game. The Aussies, meanwhile, had to grind out a win against a tough tackling French side shorn of attacking flair when their star centre Jean Marc Bourret was injured.

The two giants of world Rugby League, Australia and Great Britain, met in the final at the iconic Sydney Cricket Ground, in a match which was a battle against adversity by the British, as hooker David Ward and star winger Keith Fielding were ruled out with injury along with George Nicholls at the very last minute. Yet, with "the bionic barrel" Pitchford tormenting the Aussie defence, Great Britain went so close to victory, losing 13-12. Infamously, referee Billy Thompson ruled out a try when he blew quickly for a penalty to the British for obstruction, just as winger Stuart Wright intercepted and was running clear to the posts. And, right at the end, Fairbairn had a penalty shot to win the game which fell agonisingly short.

(Above)
Great Britain's Bill Francis in possession in the 1977 World Cup Final at the Sydney Cricket Ground against Australia.

1977 WORLD CUP RESULTS

28th May - at Carlaw Park, Auckland
AUSTRALIA beat NEW ZEALAND 27-12.
5th June - at Carlaw Park, Auckland
GREAT BRITAIN beat FRANCE 23-4.
11th June - at Sydney Cricket Ground
AUSTRALIA beat FRANCE 21-9.
12th June - at the Christchurch Show Grounds
GREAT BRITAIN beat NEW ZEALAND 30-12.
18th June - at Lang Park, Brisbane
AUSTRALIA beat GREAT BRITAIN 19-5.
19th June - at Carlaw Park, Auckland
NEW ZEALAND beat FRANCE 28-20.
The Final - 25th June - at Sydney Cricket Ground
AUSTRALIA beat GREAT BRITAIN 13-12.

70s STYLE

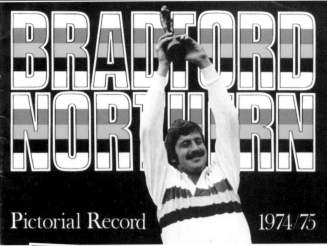

BRADFORD NORTHERN

Pictorial Record   1974/75

THIS COULD BE A **LUCKY** PROGRAMME

THE LANCASHIRE COUNTY TETLEY CUP FINAL

Salford v Swinton

Wilderspool Stadium, 21st October 1972, 3pm

Souvenir Programme   10p

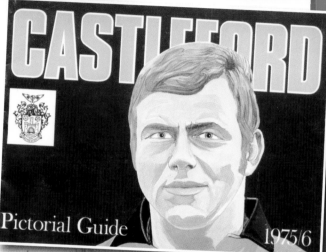

CASTLEFORD

Pictorial Guide   1975/6

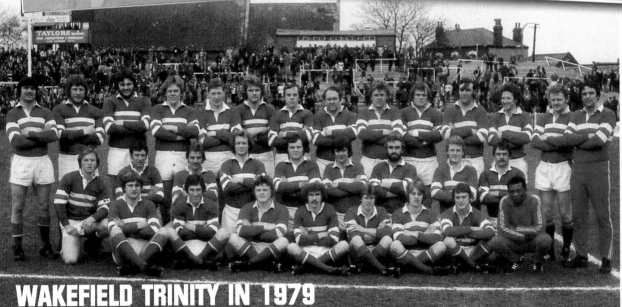

WAKEFIELD TRINITY IN 1979

The Wakefield Trinity squad in the 1978-79 season when they made it to the Challenge Cup Final and managed to revive some memories of their club's great Wembley history of the 'sixties.
29 players and every one of them British, not an overseas player in sight - and everyone wearing the same kit. They are, left to right: *(Back row):* Trevor Skerrett, Roy Bratt, Nigel Murray, Keith Rayne, Graham Brown, Dean Robinson, Graham Idle, Terry Clawson, Kevin Rayne, Brian Gregory, Bill Ashurst, Brian Juliff, John Burke, Bill Kirkbride (coach). *(Middle row):* David Needham, Les Sheard, Chris Stringer, Steve Diamond, Mike Lampkowski, David Topliss (captain), Alan McCurrie, Paul McDermott, Adrian Barwood. *(Front row):* Keith Smith, Trevor Midgley, John Thompson, Andrew Fletcher, David Wandless, Stephen Reed, Stephen Tinkler, Ben Quansah (physiotherapist).

EUROPEAN CHAMPIONSHIPS

(Right)
Centre Eric Hughes bounds over to score one of his two tries in England's 60-13 demolition of Wales at St.Helens in 1978 to clinch the Jean Galia Trophy. Other England players in the background are Stuart Wright, Paul Rose (being held by Clive Sullivan of Wales) and Geoff Pimblett. This was the rearranged game which was originally scheduled to be played in Swansea, but was postponed because of snow.

(Above)
The programme for a match that did not take place. Wales were meant to play England in Swansea in February 1978, but heavy snow caused it to be called off.

The European Championship entered the 'seventies by completing the second half of the 1969-70 tournament in which all three countries played each other home and away, although it was ironic that whilst the Wales team was made up of 100% Welshmen they were not able to play their 'home' games in the Principality. And Wales got the new decade off to a winning start with a surprise 15-11 victory over France at Perpignan, an occasion which was marred by the British referee, Dickie Thomas of Oldham, being knocked out by an angry spectator at the end of the game. That proved to be the only Welsh win in the tournament which ended with England and France level on five points each, with the English taking the Championship thanks to a better scoring average.

After 1970 the European Championship went into hibernation for four seasons as Great Britain – France Test matches made a comeback amid a general belief that there were no longer enough top quality Welsh players to form a strong national team. When the new regime entered Chapletown Road in the 1974-75 season one of their first moves was to reinstate the European Championship, playing for the Jean Galia Trophy, much to the delight of the French Rugby League who always wanted an annual international tournament to play in and present to their media and government. Plus, in an attempt to guarantee the competitiveness of the Welsh team, a new innovation allowed them to select "heritage" players based on them having at least one Welsh grandparent. That opened the door for born and bred League players – notably Bill Francis, Peter Banner and Dick Evans – to fill problem positions, and a further massive boost came for Wales when the RFL arranged for them to play on home soil for the first time in over 20 years when they lined up against France at Swansea in February 1975. Their enterprise was rewarded with a big crowd, estimated at 15,000, and a 21-8 win for a Welsh side captained by David Watkins. But it was England who retained the Championship after two close victories over France and Wales.

No European Championship was staged in the 1975-76 season because of the extended World Championships involving both England and Wales, and in 1977 it was France who finally got their hands back on the Jean Galia Trophy. With both games on their home soil, the French beat Wales solidly and then dazzled England with a spectacular show in a sometimes brutal match before a capacity crowd at Carcassonne. France, skippered by stand-off Jose Calle, discovered a new young star in centre Jean-Marc Bourret who scored two tries and five goals in the win over England. Bourret was also the key man when the French beat Wales in

1979 before a 15,000-plus crowd at Narbonne, a victory which set up a decider against England at Warrington. France, who had beaten Australia in two Tests earlier that season, were confident of adding the Euro crown, but a determined Engish team captained by Brian Lockwood just edged it 12-6.

That sealed a fourth out of five European titles for England in the 'seventies, the other being won by France. Their most spectacular win was in 1978, making up for a disastrous 1977 tournament which cost coach Peter Fox the chance to take Great Britain's World Cup team to Australasia. In 1978, with Frank Myler as coach, England - again skippered by Roger Millward - played with great spirit to beat a fired up France in the Toulouse Stadium. That two point win on French soil set up a decider against Wales, originally scheduled for Swansea but postponed because of snow. When it was played at the end of May, the English ran riot in the sunshine to score 14 tries.

(Above)
David Watkins, the Welsh captain, is left grasping thin air in the slipstream of the French centre Jean-Marc Bourret, as France beat Wales 15-8 at Narbonne in 1979. In support of Bourret is stand-off Eric Waligunda, a star of France's wins over Australia that season.

EUROPEAN CHAMPIONSHIPS IN THE 'SEVENTIES

1969-70
England 40, Wales 23. *(at Headingley)*
Wales 2, France 8. *(at Salford)*
England 11, France 11. *(at Wigan)*
France 11, Wales 15. *(at Perpignan)*
Wales 7, England 26. *(at Headingley)*
France 14, England 9. *(at Toulouse)*
Final Table: England 5pts, France 5pts, Wales 2pts.
Champions: ENGLAND

1974-75
France 9, England 11. *(at Perpignan)*
Wales 21, France 8. *(at Swansea)*
England 12, Wales 8. *(at Salford)*
Final Table: England 4pts, Wales 2pts, France 0pts.
Champions: ENGLAND

1976-77
England 2, Wales 6. *(at Headingley)*
France 13, Wales 2. *(at Toulouse)*
France 28, England 15. *(at Carcassonne)*
Final Table: France 4pts, Wales 2pts, England 0pts.
Champions: FRANCE

1977-78
Wales 29, France 7. *(at Widnes)*
France 11, England 13. *(at Toulouse)*
England 60, Wales 13. *(at St.Helens)*
Final Table: England 4pts, Wales 2pts, France 0pts.
Champions: ENGLAND

1978-79
France 15, Wales 8. *(at Narbonne)*
Wales 7, England 15. *(at Widnes)*
England 12, France 6. *(at Warrington)*
Final Table: England 4pts, France 2pts, Wales 0pts.
Champions: ENGLAND

(Left)
French prop Henri Daniel on the charge past England second-rower Phil Lowe at Toulouse in 1978. The English beat France 13-11.

FOR CLUB

Colour photographs of Rugby League action were still pretty rare during the 'Seventies, but we've tracked down the examples shown on these pages of some of the familiar colours of both the club and international game.

(Above) Kel Coslett, the St.Helens captain leads his team from the front against Salford in the 1976 Premiership Final at Swinton. The Salford defenders are hooker Dean Raistrick and second-rower Colin Dixon.

(Right) Workington Town forward Eddie Bowman proves a handful for the Widnes defence in the 1976 Lancashire Cup Final. At the end of that season, Bowman was capped by Great Britain and starred in the World Cup.

(Above) Scrums were no place for the faint-hearted, as props locked horns in their attempt to give their hooker a better chance of getting the ball. Those number nines would swing across the tunnel, paying scant notice to the written rules of scrummaging, as this action shot from a match between Warrington and Blackpool Borough at Wilderspool shows.

(Right) Much more fun for the Warrington team was posing with the local Rugby League Queen after winning the Players No.6 Trophy, among them: Tommy Martyn, Ken Kelly, John Bevan and Parry Gordon

AND COUNTRY

(Right) England captain Roger Millward, at top speed, passes to full-back Paul Charlton in the 1975 World Championship match versus France at Headingley.

(Above) Great Britain hooker Colin Clarke looks on as Ray Batten, David Topliss and Steve Nash get to grips with an Aussie in the first Test of the 1973 Ashes series at Wembley.

(Above) The distinctive battle-worn face of Mark Harris, Australia's giant centre who played in the 1970, '72, '75 and '77 World Cups. *(Below)* France versus Great Britain at Toulouse in 1971 as centre Andre Ruiz flings a pass out surrounded by British defenders Billy Benyon, John Holmes and Ken Kelly.

(Above) Alan Bates, of Dewsbury, in the 1974 Gt. Britain team.

The County Championship

(Right)
The Cumbria team which beat Yorkshire 10-7 at Workington on 11th September, 1974. Left to right: *(Back row)*: John Cunningham, Steve Hogan, John Risman, Les Gorley, Ralph Calvin, George Mather, Alan Banks, Dave Curwen, Gordon Cottier. *(Front row)*: Harry Marland, Bob Nicholson, Arnold Walker, Ian Wright, Paul Charlton, Ken Gallacher, Raymond Thompson (trainer).

(Above)
Cumberland winger Rodney Morris is chased by Lancashire forward George Nicholls in a 17-7 win for the Cumbrians at Workington in 1971. It was the last time a Cumberland team hosted the Red Rose county before the creation of the new county of Cumbria in 1973.

The County Championship saw some significant changes during the 1970s, none of which had the desired effect of attracting more support from the public - in fact, quite the opposite happened. The first big change came when the new county of Cumbria was created in 1973, causing Barrow to switch allegience from Lancashire to their Cumbrian 'neighbours' from further up the north west coast. Not only did the new Cumbria team then include Barrovians, but by the mid-'seventies they also opened their doors to outsiders who were not born in the county but happened to be playing for one of its three professional clubs. This resulted in Welshmen (including Gordon Pritchard, Chris Camilleri and Ray Wilkins) representing Cumbria, along with several Lancastrians, notably Iain MacCorquodale, Ian Ball and Steve Tickle.

Lancashire also followed this trend by selecting Midlanders Keith Fielding and Mike Coulman, plus the Welsh international wing John Bevan. In contrast, Yorkshire - under the steadfast influence of their county secretary the redoubtable 'George' Hirst - maintained their tradition of selecting only Yorkshire-born players. The changes didn't help the Cumbrian team, as they went throughout the 'seventies without a single County Championship title, in contrast to the previous decade when they were top dog ahead of both Lancashire and Yorkshire. Things weren't quite as bad as that might sound for the Cumbrians in the 1970s, as on five occasions they finished in level first place, only to lose out on points-scoring differences when it came to deciding the champions - and they also took Yorkshire to a play-off decider at Leeds in the 1972-73 season. The 'seventies saw the white rose county win five of the nine available County Championship titles, ahead of Lancashire's four. No Championship was played during the Queen's Jubilee year of 1977. A major innovation was the introduction of an Other Nationalities side in 1974-75 - a mixture of overseas players and those not born in the three established counties. It didn't catch on, lasting for only two seasons, and with the County games being moved from their traditional early season slot, some pitifully small attendances bothered to watch - the nadir coming when just 737 people were scattered around the vast Odsal bowl to see Yorkshire play Other Nationalities on a December Saturday in 1975.

(Above) **Not a single spectator in sight at Odsal Stadium as Yorkshire played the Other Nationalities on 6th December, 1975. The two sides fought out an exciting 16-all draw, and the man in possession is Frank Wilson, with Aussies Bruce Gibbs and Steve Martin in closest support. Yorkhire players are, from left to right: Bob Irving, Steve Norton, Jimmy Thompson (on the floor tackling Wilson) and Steve Nash.**

COUNTY CHAMPIONSHIPS IN THE 'SEVENTIES

1970-71
Cumberland 21, Yorkshire 15. *(at Whitehaven)*
Lancashire 28, Cumberland 5. *(at Barrow)*
Yorkshire 32, Lancashire 12. *(at Castleford)*
Play-off: Yorkshire 34, Lancashire 8. *(at Catsleford)*
Champions: YORKSHIRE

1971-72
Cumberland 17, Lancashire 7. *(at Workington)*
Lancashire 22, Yorkshire 42. *(at Leigh)*
Yorkshire 17, Cumberland 12. *(at Wakefield)*
Champions: YORKSHIRE

1972-73
Cumberland 23, Yorkshire 14. *(at Whitehaven)*
Lancashire 26, Cumberland 16. *(at Warrington)*
Yorkshire 32, Lancashire 18. *(at Castleford)*
Play-off: Yorkshire 20, Cumberland 7. *(at Leeds)*
Champions: YORKSHIRE

1973-74
Cumbria 6, Lancashire 18. *(at Barrow)*
Yorkshire 37, Cumbria 12. *(at Bramley)*
Lancashire 17, Yorkshire 15. *(at Widnes)*
Champions: LANCASHIRE

1974-75
Lancashire 14, Other Nationalities 13. *(at Salford)*
Cumbria 10, Yorkshire 7. *(at Workington)*
Lancashire 29, Cumbria 4. *(at Warrington)*
Yorkshire 22, Other Nationalities 15. *(at Hull K.R.)*
Yorkshire 20, Lancashire 14. *(at Keighley)*
Cumbria 19, Other Nationalities 12. *(at Whitehaven)*
Play-off: Lancashire 29, Yorkshire 11. *(at Widnes)*
Champions: LANCASHIRE

1975-76
Yorkshire 10, Cumbria 7. *(at Dewsbury)*
Lancashire 36, Other Nationalities 7. *(at St.Helens)*
Lancashire 7, Yorkshire 17. *(at Wigan)*
Cumbria 21, Other Nationalities 13. *(at Barrow)*
Cumbria 17, Lancashire 22. *(at Workington)*
Yorkshire 16, Other Nationalities 16. *(at Bradford)*
Champions: YORKSHIRE

1976-77
Lancashire 18, Cumbria 14.
(at Leigh)
Cumbria 12, Yorkshire 12.
(at Whitehaven)
Yorkshire 18, Lancashire 13.
(at Castleford)
Champions: YORKSHIRE

1977-78
County Championship not held: - instead Silver Jubilee Fund County games were played:
Yorkshire 28, Cumbria 10. *(at York)*
Lancashire 33, Yorkshire 8. *(at Widnes)*

1978-79
Yorkshire 37, Cumbria 9. *(at the Boulevard, Hull)*
Lancashire 23, Yorkshire 7. *(at Widnes)*
Cumbria 16, Lancashire 15. *(at Whitehaven)*
Champions: LANCASHIRE

1979-80
Cumbria 17, Yorkshire 13. *(at Workington)*
Lancashire 23, Cumbria 15. *(at St.Helens)*
Yorkshire 19, Lancashire 16. *(at Castleford)*
Champions: LANCASHIRE

MURPHY MAGIC

In the first half of the 'Seventies the game had no bigger winner than Alex Murphy.

THE RUGBY LEAGUE CHALLENGE CUP COMPETITION

FINAL

SATURDAY, 15th MAY, 1971 Kick-off 3p.m.

LEEDS v LEIGH

Official Programme . . . 10p

EMPIRE **WEMBLEY** STADIUM

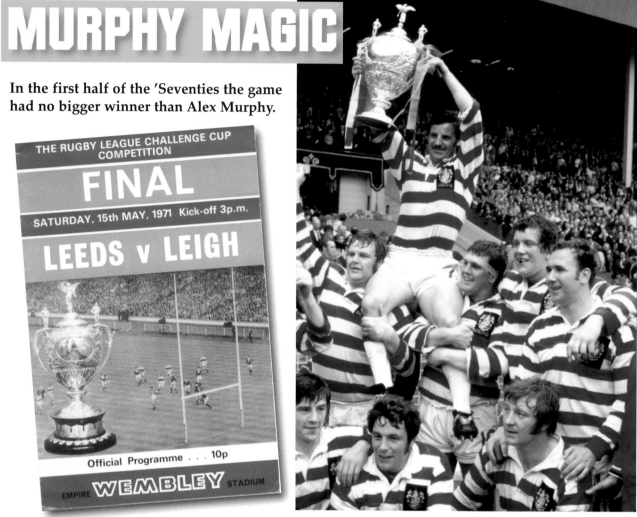

(Above) Alex made a Wembley dream come true for Leigh in 1971, in their one and only appearance in front of the twin towers. Murphy was the brains behind Leigh's crushing win over favourites Leeds, taking the Lance Todd Trophy, being carried off on a stretcher, and returning to carry the Cup aloft.

(Above) Soon after achieving glory with Leigh, Alex left for Warrington where he built a new dynasty as the Wire became one of the dominant sides of the 'Seventies, winning at Wembley in 1974 along with many other trophies. The Warrington team of 1975 is pictured here with coach Murphy on the far right.

UNION INTERNATIONALS IN LEAGUE

(Above, left to right) **Keith Smith (Wakefield Trinity), Mike Lampkowski (Wakefield Trinity) and Keith Fielding (Salford) - three 1970s England Rugby Union internationals who made a successful transition to League.**

There were no financial constraints on League clubs in the 'seventies when it came to chasing the signatures of players from Rugby Union, but there was a surprising shift in emphasis as more English R.U. caps crossed the divide than Welsh. Of the seven England internationals signed by League clubs, four were forwards - but it was the three backs who were the biggest successes - Yorkshiremen Keith Smith and Mike Lampkowski with Wakefield Trinity, and midlander Keith Fielding at Salford. Fielding had a phenomenal impact on his new game, finishing his first season as the league's top try-scorer and scoring a hat-trick in his Great Britain Test debut. The biggest name from Rugby Union was Welsh winger John Bevan, one of the stars from the famous 1971 Lions tour - another of those tourists, 'Chico' Hopkins also came to League but his signing proved to be an expensive flop for Swinton. Most inspired recruit was Irishman Ken Goodall by Workington - he was a great natural League player whose career was cut short by injury.

(Above)
Ken Goodall, the Irish Rugby Union forward, pictured on the day he was introduced to the press as a Workington Town player in the summer of 1970, wearing the full Springbok kit he had obtained whilst on a Lions tour to South Africa. Ulsterman Goodall was a natural in Rugby League.

HOME NATIONS R.U. INTERNATIONALS SIGNED IN THE 'SEVENTIES

England
Keith Fairbrother - signed by Leigh, 1974-75
(Coventry - 12 caps)
Keith Fielding - signed by Salford, 1973-74
(Moseley - 10 caps)
Mike Lampkowski - signed by Wakefield, 1976-77
(Headingley - 4 caps)
Mike Leadbetter - signed by Rochdale, 1974-75
(Broughton Park - 1 cap)
Bob Mordell - signed by Oldham, 1979-80
(Rosslyn Park - 1 cap)
Keith Smith - signed by Wakefield, 1977-78
(Roundhay - 4 caps)
Bryan West - signed by Wakefield, 1970-71
(Northampton - 8 caps)

Ireland
Ken Goodall - signed by Workington, 1970-71
(Derry - 19 caps)

Wales
John Bevan - signed by Warrington, 1973-74
(Cardiff - 10 caps, plus 1 British Lions cap)
Stuart Gallacher - signed by Bradford, 1970-71
(Llanelli -1 cap)
Clive Griffiths - signed by St.Helens, 1979-80
(Llanelli - 1 cap)
Ray 'Chico' Hopkins - signed by Swinton, 1972-73
(Maesteg - 1 cap, plus 1 British Lions cap)
Roy Mathias - signed by St.Helens, 1972-73
(Llanelli - 1 cap)
Glyn Shaw - signed by Widnes, 1977-78
(Neath - 12 caps)

CHALLENGE CUP FINALS

(Right)
George Nicholls in possession in what was undoubtedly the best Cup Final seen at Wembley during the 'seventies. This was the 1978 epic in which St.Helens forward Nicholls was named as the Lance Todd Trophy winner before John Holmes turned the game around brilliantly for Leeds. The Loiners came back to win 14-12 in front of a crowd of 95,872.

(Above)
Castleford retained the Cup in 1970 and skipper Alan Hardisty celebrates at Wembley alongside the newcomer in their team - Lance Todd Trophy winner Bill Kirkbride

Castleford kicked off what proved to be an epic decade for Challenge Cup Finals by retaining the trophy they had won in 1969, beating Wigan at Wembley in a low scoring match which left the Lancastrians with much to feel aggrieved about. Over 95,000 people were there to see the 1970 final as the game's showpiece event in front of Wembley's twin towers continued to grow into one of the nation's favourite sporting events - and, as soccer became more and more bedevilled by hooliganism, an image of the "friendly final" gave Rugby League a feelgood factor embellished by traditional pre-match community singing and colourful marching bands.

In contrast, Alex Murphy brought an air of hard-nosed professionalism to Wembley as he dominated the game's biggest stage. After being a winner there with St.Helens in the 'sixties, Alex returned as player-coach with Leigh in 1971, then Warrington in '74, to lift the Challenge Cup again in two finals surrounded by controversies. Leigh's triumph against Leeds provided one of Wembley's biggest upsets on a day when Syd Hynes became the first man to be sent off at Wembley following an "incident" with Murphy; and when Alex captained Warrington to their first Challenge Cup for twenty years in 1974, the Wire won few friends in a display marred by gamesmanship and foul play which left opponents Featherstone battered, bruised and beaten. In pleasant contrast for the Rovers, the year before they had enjoyed a wonderful day at Wembley as they produced some glorious attacking rugby to outclass Bradford Northern and take the Cup back to Post Office Road.

Captained by the stylish John Newlove and with the effervescent Steve Nash at scrum-half, Featherstone turned on a master class of moves from the coaching book of Peter Fox. That orgy of points scoring at Wembley came in sharp contrast to a tense and very close battle between St.Helens and Leeds the year before when the goal-kicking of Kel Coslett won the Cup, as Leeds prop Terry Clawson was left to rue some missed kicks.

Widnes emerged as the top cup fighting team of the 'seventies, with four Wembley finals - two won and two lost; but it was Leeds who put the seal on the decade with victory in two epic Cup Finals, in 1977 against Widnes and '78 against St.Helens. It was Wembley joy at last for the Loiners after they had suffered such disappointments there in 1971 and '72, and due reward for the quality of players like John Holmes, David Ward and Les Dyl.

(Right) **Featherstone Rovers full-back Cyril Kellett slots his eighth goal from eight attempts at Wembley in 1973, as the Rovers hammered Bradford Northern 33-14 to take the Cup.**

CHALLENGE CUP FINALS IN THE 'SEVENTIES

1970
Saturday 9th May 1970, at Wembley Stadium
Castleford 7, Wigan 2.
Castleford: Try: Lowndes.
Goal: Redfearn (2).
Wigan: Goal: Tyrer.
CASTLEFORD: D.Edwards: T.Briggs, A.Thomas, I.Stenton, A.Lowndes; A.Hardisty, K.Hepworth; D.Hartley, C.Dickinson, M.Redfearn, W.Kirkbride, B.Lockwood, M.Reilly. *Sub.:* D.Hargrave (for Hardisty).
WIGAN: C.Tyrer;. K.Jones, W.Francis, P.Rowe, Kevin O'Loughlin; D.Hill, F.Parr; K.Ashcroft, R.Burdell, B.Hogan, W.Ashurst, D.Robinson, D.Laughton. *Sub.:* C.Hill (for Tyrer).
Referee: Mr. G.F. Lindop (Wakefield)
Attendance: 95,255. Receipts: £89,262..

1971
Saturday 15th May 1971, at Wembley Stadium
Leigh 24, Leeds 7.
Leigh: Tries: Dorrington, Eckersley.
Goals: Ferguson (5), Murphy (2), Eckersley, Fiddler.
Leeds: Try: Wainwright. Goals: Holmes (2).
LEIGH: D.Eckersley; S.Ferguson, S.Dorrington, M.Collins, J.Walsh; A.Barrow, A.Murphy; D.Watts, K.Ashcroft, J.Fiddler, G.Clarkson, P.Grimes, P.Smethurst. *Sub.:* L.Chisnall (for Murphy).
LEEDS: J.Holmes; J.Langley, S.Hynes, R.Cowan, J.Atkinson; A.Wainwright, B.Seabourne; J.Burke, A.Fisher, T.Barnard, D.Hick, R.Haigh, R.Batten. *Sub.:* L.Dyl (for Cowan).
Referee: Mr. W.H. Thompson (Huddersfield)
Attendance: 84,641. Receipts: £84,402.

1972
Saturday 11th May 1972, at Wembley Stadium
St.Helens 16, Leeds 13.
St.Helens: Tries: Rees, Jones. Goals: Coslett (5).
Leeds: Try: Cookson. Goals: Clawson (5).
ST.HELENS: G.Pimblett; L.Jones, W.Benyon, J.Walsh, F.Wilson; K.Kelly, J.Heaton; G.Rees, L.Greenall, J.Stephens, J.Mantle, E.Chisnall, K.Coslett. *No subs. used.*
LEEDS: J.Holmes; A.Smith, S.Hynes, L.Dyl, J.Atkinson; A.Hardisty, K.Hepworth; T.Clawson, A.Fisher, W.Ramsey, P.Cookson, R.Haigh, R.Batten. *Sub.:* J.Langley (for Hynes).
Referee: Mr. E. Lawrinson (Warrington).
Attendance: 89,495. Receipts: £86,361.

1973
Saturday 12th May 1973, at Wembley Stadium
Featherstone R. 33, Bradford N. 14.
Featherstone: Tries: Newlove (2), Smith, Farrar, Hartley. Goals: Kellett (8), Nash.
Bradford: Tries: Redfearn, Fearnley. Goals: Tees (4).
FEATHERSTONE ROVERS: C.Kellett; P.Coventry, M.Smith, J.Newlove, K.Kellett; M.Mason, S.Nash; L.Tonks, K.Bridges, V.Farrar, A.Rhodes, J.Thompson, R.Stone. *Subs.:* D.Hartley (for Smith), B.Hollis (for Rhodes).
BRADFORD NORTHERN E.Tees; M.Lamb, D.Stockwell, B.Watson, A.Redfearn; M.Blacker, B.Seabourne; B.Hogan, P.Dunn, K.Earl, G.Joyce, W.Pattinson, S.Fearnley. *Subs.:* D.Treasure (for Blacker), A.Long (for Earl).
Referee: Mr. M.J. Naughton (Widnes)
Attendance: 72,395. Receipts: £125,826.

It was certainly the Cup that cheered in the 'seventies, as these moments of celebration show for St.Helens in 1976, Leeds in 1978 and Widnes in 1979. All three of these clubs were no strangers to Wembley throughout the decade, and their captains on these occasions: Kel Coslett, David Ward and Reg Bowden, got used to picking up silverware. The Saints victory over Widnes in 1976 was probably their most satisfying as it came against all the odds.

1974

Saturday 11th May 1974, at Wembley Stadium.
Warrington 24, Featherstone R. 9
Warrington: Tries: Ashcroft, Nicholas..
Goals: Whitehead (7), Murphy (2).
Featherstone: Try: Newlove. Goals: Box (3).
WARRINGTON: D.Whitehead; M.Philbin, D.Noonan, A.Whittle, J.Bevan; A.Murphy, P.Gordon; D.Chisnall, K.Ashcroft, B.Brady, D.Wright, M.Nicholas, B.Philbin. *Subs.:* W.Pickup (for Murphy), R.Wanbon (for Brady).
FEATHERSTONE ROVERS: H.Box; D.Dyas, M.Smith, D.Hartley, G.Bray; J.Newlove, S.Nash; L.Tonks, K.Bridges, W.Harris, A.Rhodes, J.Thompson, K.Bell. *Subs.:* D.Busfield (for Rhodes), R.Stone (for Thompson).
Referee: Mr. S. Shepherd (Oldham).
Attendance: 76,411. Receipts: £132,021.

1975

Saturday 10th May 1975, at Wembley Stadium.
Widnes 14, Warrington 7.
Widnes: Try: Mills.
Goals: Dutton 5. Drop-goal: Dutton.
Warrington: Try: Bevan. Goals: Whitehead (2).
WIDNES: R.Dutton; A.Prescott, M.George, M.Aspey, C.Anderson; E.Hughes, R.Bowden; J.Mills, K.Elwell, B.Sheridan, J.Foran, M.Adams, D.Laughton. *No subs. used.*
WARRINGTON: D.Whitehead; M.Philbin,

D.Noonan, F.Reynolds, J.Bevan; A.Whittle, P.Gordon; D.Chisnall, K.Ashcroft, R.Wanbon, T.Conroy, T.Martyn, B.Philbin. *Subs.:* W.Briggs (for Reynolds), M.Nicholas (for Martyn).
Referee: Mr. P. Geraghty (York).
Attendance: 86,363. Receipts: £140,732.

1976

Saturday 8th May 1976, at Wembley Stadium.
St.Helens 20, Widnes 5.
St.Helens: Tries: Glynn (2), Cunningham, Heaton.
Goals: Pimblett (3).
Drop-goals: Pimblett (2).

(Above) **Jeff Heaton's try for St.Helens in 1976.**

Widnes: Goals: Dutton (2). Drop-goal: Elwell.
ST.HELENS: G.Pimblett; L.Jones, E.Cunningham, D.Noonan, R.Mathias; W.Benyon, J.Heaton; J.Mantle, A.Karalius, K.Coslett, G.Nicholls, E.Chisnall, D.Hull. *Subs.:* P.Glynn (for Benyon), M.James (for Mantle).
WIDNES: R.Dutton; A.Prescott, E.Hughes, M.George, D.Jenkins; D.Eckersley, R.Bowden; N.Nelson, K.Elwell, J.Wood, J.Foran, M.Adams, D.Laughton. *Subs.:* D.O'Neill (for Prescott), B.Sheridan (for Foran).
Referee: Mr. R. Moore (Wakefield).
Attendance: 89,982. Receipts: £190,129.

(Above) Widnes stand-off Eric Hughes touches down for the Chemics' second try to seal victory in the 1979 Challenge Cup Final. Wakefield Trinity prop Trevor Skerrett and referee Joe Jackson are closest to the try.

1977

Saturday 7th May 1977, at Wembley Stadium

Leeds 16, Widnes 7.

Leeds: Tries: *Atkinson, Dyl, Dick.*
Goals: *Dick (3).* **Drop-goal:** *Dick.*
Widnes: Try: *Aspey.* **Goals:** *Dutton (2).*
LEEDS: .B.Murrell; A.Smith, N.Hague, L.Dyl, J.Atkinson; J.Holmes, K.Dick; M.Harrison, D.Ward, S.Pitchford, G.Eccles, P.Cookson, S.Fearnley. **Subs.:** D.Smith (for A.Smith), R.Dickinson (for Fearnley).
WIDNES: R.Dutton; S.Wright, M.Aspey, D.Eckersley, D.O'Neill; E.Hughes, R.Bowden; W.Ramsey, K.Elwell, J.Mills, A.Dearden, M.Adams, D.Laughton. **Subs.:** M.George (for Wright), J.Foran (for Dearden).
Referee: *Mr. J.V. Moss (Manchester).*
Attendance: *80,871.* **Receipts:** *£241,487.*

1978

Saturday 13th May 1978, at Wembley Stadium.

Leeds 14, St.Helens 12.

Leeds: Tries: *Atkinson, Smith, Cookson.*
Goal: *Oulton.* **Drop-goals:** *Ward (2), Holmes.*
St.Helens: Tries: *Liptrot, Francis.* **Goals:** *Pimblett (3).*
LEEDS: W.Oulton; D.Smith, N.Hague, L.Dyl, J.Atkinson; J.Holmes, J.Sanderson; M.Harrison, D.Ward, S.Pitchford, G.Eccles, P.Cookson, M.Crane. **Subs.:** K.Dick (for Sanderson), R.Dickinson (for Harrison).

ST.HELENS: G.Pimblett; L.Jones, D.Noonan, P.Glynn, R.Mathias; W.Francis; K.Gwilliam; D.Chisnall, G.Liptrot, M.James, G.Nicholls, E.Cunningham, H. Pinner. *No subs. used.*
Referee: *Mr. W.H. Thompson (Huddersfield).*
Attendance: *95,872.*
Receipts: *£330,573.*

(Above) Kevin Dick, starred for Leeds at Wembley in 1977.

1979

Saturday 5th May 1979, at Wembley Stadium.

Widnes 12, Wakefield Trinity 3.

Widnes: Tries: *Wright, Hughes.*
Goals: *Burke (2).* **Drop-goals:** *Eckersley, Elwell.*
Wakefield Trinity: Try: *Fletcher.*
WIDNES: D.Eckersley; S.Wright, M.Aspey, M.George, M.Burke; E.Hughes, R.Bowden; J.Mills, K.Elwell, G.Shaw, M.Adams, A.Dearden, D.Laughton. **Subs.:** D.Hull (for George), M.O'Neill (for Dearden).
WAKEFIELD TRINITY: L.Sheard; A.Fletcher, K.Smith, S.Diamond, B.Juliffe; D.Topliss, M.Lampkowski; J.Burke, A.McCurrie, T.Skerrett, W.Ashurst, Keith Rayne, G.Idle. *No subs. used.*
Referee: *Mr. J. Jackson (Pudsey).*
Attendance: *94,218.* **Receipts:** *£383,157.*

CHAMPIONSHIP FINALS

The first four seasons of the 'seventies saw the last of Northern Rugby League's traditional Championship Finals, when the title was contested by all thirty clubs who played together in one big league, before the introduction of two divisions in 1973-74 changed things forever.

(Above)
St.Helens captain Kel Coslett raises the trophy in 1971 at Station Road as the Saints retained the Championship. On the picture are, left to right: Coach Jim Challinor, Ken Kelly, Bob Blackwood, Jeff Heaton, Bobby Wanbon, Graham Rees, John Stephens, Alan Whittle and Les Jones.

Those four seasons also saw the top-16 play-off system used for the last time to decide the Champions and, significantly, on only one occasion (Leeds in 1972) did the team which finished as league leaders go on to win the Championship Final. The Loiners had been hot favourites for the title in 1970 when they finished top of the league and played spectacular attacking football as they swept through the play-offs; but they reckoned without a resolute St.Helens team who dominated them in the final at Odsal Stadium. On a mid May afternoon which saw the British weather deliver all four seasons in the space of an hour – from warm and sunny to torrential rain and hail-storms – the Saints were inspired by Frank Myler, who very soon after departed for Australia as captain of the 1970 Lions touring team. The Leeds performance featured a spectacular solo try by Scotsman Ron Cowan, but that could not stop St.Helens going on to have their captain Cliff Watson lift the Championship trophy.

Saints retained that trophy a year later when they beat league leaders Wigan at Station Road thanks to a late, and rather fortuitous, try by Billy Benyon. And they were back at Swinton for a third consecutive Championship Final in 1972 when they lined up against Leeds just seven days after they had beaten them at Wembley to win the Challenge Cup. The Loiners got their revenge, and especially their prop-forward Terry Clawson whose missed goal-kicks cost his side so dearly at Wembley. In the Championship Final Terry rediscovered his kicking form and his vital contribution to the Leeds win brought him the Harry Sunderland Trophy as man of the match.

The very last Championship Final in 1973 brought its most romantic story as Dewsbury won the title for the first time in their history. "Little" Dewsbury came from eight place in the league table and turned on a spectacular display to overcome Leeds 22-13 in the final at Odsal Stadium. With the two Stephensons (no relation) – Nigel and Mick – their two great tacticians, ably supported by other quality footballers like Allan Agar and Alan Bates working behind a mighty pack, Dewsbury's coach Tommy Smales had them pulling off intricate moves to perfection which bamboozled the Leeds defence and brought four tries. Outside of Headingley, there was a never a more popular victory in a Championship Final.

(Above, left) Dewsbury hooker Mick Stephenson dives over to score the second of his two tries in the 1973 Championship Final and *(above, right)* with the trophy in the dressing room at Odsal after their stunning victory over Leeds which brought Dewsbury the title and Stephenson the Harry Sunderland Trophy.

CHAMPIONSHIP FINALS IN THE 'SEVENTIES

1970
Saturday 16th May 1970, at Odsal Stadium, Bradford.
St.Helens 24, Leeds 12.
St.Helens: Tries: Prescott (2), Walsh, Sayer.
Goals: Coslett (4), Walsh (2).
Leeds: Tries: Hynes, Cowan. Goals: Holmes (3).
ST.HELENS: F.Barrow; L.Jones, W.Benyon, J.Walsh, E.Prescott; F.Myler, J.Heaton; A.Halsall, W.Sayer, C.Watson, J.Mantle, E.Chisnall, K.Coslett. *No subs.*
LEEDS: J.Holmes; A.Smith, S.Hynes, R.Cowan, J.Atkinson; M.Shoebottom, B.Seabourne; J.Burke, A.Crosby, A.Eyre, W.Ramsey, G.Eccles, R.Batten.
Sub.: D.Hick (for Ramsey).
Referee: Mr. W.H. Thompson (Huddersfield).
Attendance: 26,358. Receipts: £9,301.

1971
Saturday 22nd May 1971, at Station Road, Swinton.
St.Helens 16, Wigan 12.
St.Helens: Tries: Blackwood, Benyon.
Goals: Coslett (5).
Wigan: Tries: Ashurst, Robinson.
Goals: Ashurst (2), Tyrer.
ST.HELENS: G.Pimblett; L.Jones, W.Benyon, J.Walsh, R.Blackwood; A.Whittle, J.Heaton; J.Stephens, A.Karalius, G.Rees, J.Mantle, E.Chisnall, K.Coslett.
Subs.: K.Kelly (for Benyon), R.Wanbon (for Rees).
WIGAN: C.Tyrer; Kevin O'Loughlin, W.Francis, P.Rowe, S.Wright; D.Hill, W.Ayres; B.Hogan, C.Clarke, G.Fletcher, W.Ashurst, D.Robinson, D.Laughton. *Sub.: E.Cunningham (for Robinson).*
Referee: Mr. E. Lawrinson (Warrington).
Attendance: 21,745. Receipts: £10,201.

1972
Saturday 20th May 1972, at Station Road, Swinton.
Leeds 9, St.Helens 5.
Leeds: Try: Atkinson. Goals: Clawson (3).
St.Helens: Try: Greenall. Goal: Walsh.
LEEDS: J.Holmes; A.Smith, J.Langley, L.Dyl, J.Atkinson; A.Hardisty, D.Barham; T.Clawson, D.Ward, A.Fisher, P.Cookson, G.Eccles, R.Batten.
Subs.: D.Hick (for Fisher), P.Pickup (for Holmes).
ST.HELENS: G.Pimblett; L.Jones, W.Benyon, J.Walsh, F.Wilson; K.Kelly, J.Heaton; G.Rees, L.Greenall, J.Stephens, J.Mantle, E.Chisnall, K.Coslett. *Sub.: A.Whittle (for Jones).*
Referee: Mr. S. Shepherd (Oldham).
Attendance: 24,055. Receipts: £9,513.

1973
Saturday 19th May 1973, at Odsal Stadium, Bradford.
Dewsbury 22, Leeds 13.
Dewsbury: Tries: Mick Stephenson (2), Nigel Stephenson, Agar.
Goals: Nigel Stephenson (5).
Leeds: Tries: Dyl, Cookson, Eccles.
Goals: Clawson, Hynes.
DEWSBURY: A.Rushton; G.Ashcroft, J.Clark, Nigel Stephenson, T.Day; A.Agar, Alan Bates; H.Beverley, Mick Stephenson, T.Lowe, J.Grayshon, John Bates, J.Whittingham. *Sub.: B.Taylor (for Beverley).*
LEEDS: J.Holmes; A.Smith, S.Hynes, L.Dyl, J.Atkinson; A.Hardisty, K.Hepworth; T.Clawson, A.Fisher, G.Clarkson, P.Cookson, G.Eccles, R.Haigh.
Subs.: J.Langley (for Clarkson), D.Ward (for Fisher).
Referee: Mr. H.G. Hunt (Prestbury).
Attendance: 18,889. Receipts: £9,479.

PREMIERSHIP FINALS

(Right)
Happy faces in the St.Helens dressing room at Station Road in 1977, after the Saints win over Warrington in the Premiership Final. Skipper Billy Benyon holds the trophy, alongside full-back Geoff Pimblett with the Harry Sunderland trophy after being chosen as the man of the match. Saints won 32-20 in scorching conditions.

(Above)
The Rugby Football League's 'new look' programme for the very first Premiership Final in 1975.

Since 1907 the Championship had been decided with a top-four play off at the end of each season (which became the top-16 in 1965) and the popularity of the financially lucrative Championship Final had remained one of the arguments used against the idea of splitting the league into two divisions. When two divisions came to stay in 1973-74 there was, in theory, no need for the game to continue with Championship play-offs, however, it decided to create a new style end of season play-off. But, like so many things in Rugby League, it took a while for logic to take hold.

At the end of the 1973-74 season, with Salford crowned as Champions, a convoluted tournament called "The Club Championship" was introduced in which, in theory, every club except the bottom two of the second division could end up winning. In the event Warrington won it in what was a highly successful season for them, beating St.Helens in the final – but nobody really understood how they got there!

The following year, 1974-75, the Premiership was born – but involving the top 12 first division teams plus the top four from Division Two. Leeds were the first winners, beating St.Helens 26-11 in the final. It was to be 1975-76 before Rugby League finally stuck on the idea of an end of season Premiership involving the top eight teams in the first division – St.Helens winning the final against Salford 15-2, as the unlucky Red Devils once again came up short in knockout football after being crowned Championship winners. And from then on, the Premiership Final became a cherished end of season event and, because it was always televised by the BBC, the winners usually found themselves getting more kudos than the actual Champions who deserved it. Remarkably, not once in every season of the decade after two divisions were introduced in 1973-74, did the Champions go on to win the Premiership title.

Scorching weather and bone-hard pitches were the norm for Premiership Finals. St.Helens retained the title in 1977 in a high scoring win over Warrington as Station Road became the favoured venue. Bradford Northern beat Champions Widnes to win it in 1978 before meeting Yorkshire rivals Leeds at Fartown the following year - players from both clubs delayed leaving for the 1979 Lions tour to take part as the Loiners won by a suprisingly big margin.

(Left) **Warrington hooker Kevin Ashcroft chaired by the fans after the Wire's victory over St.Helens in the 1974 Club Championship Final at Central Park.**

PREMIERSHIP FINALS IN THE 'SEVENTIES

1974 *(Club Championship Final)*
Saturday 18th May 1974, at Central Park, Wigan.
Warrington 13, St.Helens 12.
Warrington: Tries: Mike Philbin, Noonan, Brady.
Goals: Whitehead (2).
St.Helens: Tries: Wilson (2). Goals: Coslett (3).
WARRINGTON: D.Whitehad; M.Philbin, D.Noonan, W.Pickup, J.Bevan; A.Whittle, A.Murphy; D.Chisnall, K.Ashcroft, B.Brady, R.Wanbon, I.Mather, B.Philbin.
Subs.: J.Lowe (for Pickup), W.Gaskell (for Wanbon).
ST.HELENS: G.Pimblett; D.Brown, J.Wills, F.Wilson, R.Mathias; D.Eckersley, J.Heaton; J.Mantle, G.Liptrot, M.Murphy, E,Chisnall, G.Nicholls, K.Coslett. *Sub.: J.Warlow (for Chisnall).*
Referee: Mr. P. Geraghty (York).
Attendance: 18,040. Receipts: £10,031.

1975
Saturday 17th May 1975, at Central Park, Wigan.
Leeds 26, St.Helens 11.
Leeds: Tries: Atkinson (2), Smith, Hynes, Mason.
Goals: Holmes (2). Drop-goal: Hynes.
St.Helens: Tries: Jones, Mathias, Heaton.
Goal: Coslett.
LEEDS: J.Holmes; A.Smith, S.Hynes, L.Dyl, J.Atkinson; M.Mason, K.Hepworth; R.Dickinson, D.Ward, S.Pitchford, P.Cookson, R.Batten, R.Haigh.
Subs.: D.Marshall (for Holmes), G.Eccles (for Hynes).
ST.HELENS: G.Pimblett; L.Jones, F.Wilson, D.Hull, R.Mathias; J.Walsh, J.Heaton; J.Warlow, A.Karalius, J.Mantle, E.Chisnall, G.Nicholls, K.Coslett.
Subs.: K.Gwilliam (for Mantle), E.Cunningham (for Warlow).
Referee: Mr. W.H. Thompson (Huddersfield).
Attendance: 14,531. Receipts: £8,401.

1976
Saturday 22nd May 1976, at Station Road, Swinton.
St.Helens 15, Salford 2.
St.Helens: Tries: Glynn, Karalius, Chisnall.
Goals: Pimblett (3).
Salford: Drop-goals: Watkins (2).
ST.HELENS: G.Pimblett; L.Jones, P.Glynn, D.Noonan, R.Mathias; W.Benyon, J.Heaton; J.Mantle, A.Karalius, M.James, G.Nicholls, E.Chisnall, K.Coslett. *Sub.: K.Gwilliam (for Heaton).*
SALFORD: D.Watkins; K.Fielding, M.Richards, C.Hesketh, G.Graham; J.Butler, S.Nash; M.Coulman, D.Raistrick, W.Sheffield, J.Knighton, C.Dixon, E.Prescott. *Sub.: S.Turnbull (for Knighton).*
Referee: Mr. M.J. Naughton (Widnes).
Attendance: 18,082. Receipts: £13,138.

1977
Saturday 28th May 1977, at Station Road, Swinton.
St.Helens 32, Warrington 20.
St.Helens: Tries: Pimblett, Benyon, Cunningham, James, Mathias, Ken Gwilliam.Goals: Pimblett (7).
Warrington: Tries: Alan Gwilliam, Gordon, Weavill, Philbin. Goals: Hesford (4).
ST.HELENS: G.Pimblett; L.Jones, W.Benyon, E.Cunningham, R.Mathias; P.Glynn, K.Gwilliam; D.Chisnall, G.Liptrot, M.James, G.Nicholls, E.Chisnall, H.Pinner. *Subs.: A.Ashton (for Glynn), A.Karalius (for Nicholls).*
WARRINGTON: D.Finnigan; D.Curling, J.Bevan, S.Hesford, M.Kelly; A.Gwilliam, P.Gordon; D.Weavill, J.Price, B.Case, R.Lester, T.Martyn, B.Philbin
Subs.: M.Peers (for Martyn), D.Cunliffe (for Bevan).
Referee: Mr. G.F. Lindop (Wakefield).
Attendance: 11,507. Receipts: £11,625.

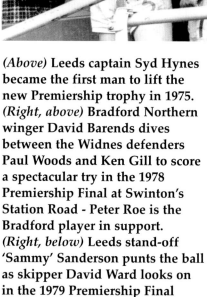

(Above) Leeds captain Syd Hynes became the first man to lift the new Premiership trophy in 1975.
(Right, above) Bradford Northern winger David Barends dives between the Widnes defenders Paul Woods and Ken Gill to score a spectacular try in the 1978 Premiership Final at Swinton's Station Road - Peter Roe is the Bradford player in support.
(Right, below) Leeds stand-off 'Sammy' Sanderson punts the ball as skipper David Ward looks on in the 1979 Premiership Final played at Fartown. Bradford second-rower Jeff Grayshon tries to charge down as Leeds won 24-2.

1978

Saturday 20th May 1978, at Station Road, Swinton.
Bradford Northern 17, Widnes 8.
Bradford: Tries: Barends, Roe, David Redefearn, Haigh.
Goals: Mumby (2). Drop-goal: Wolford.
Widnes: Tries: Aspey (2). Goal: Woods.
BRADFORD NORTHERN: K.Mumby; D.Barends, P.Roe, J.Austin, D.Redfearn; J.Wolford, A.Redfearn; I.Van Bellen, D.Raistrick, J.Thompson, G.Joyce, D.Trotter, R.Haigh.
Subs.: N.Fox (for Van Bellen), C.Forsyth (for Joyce).
WIDNES: D.Eckersely; S.Wright, E.Hughes, M.Aspey, P.Woods; K.Gill, R.Bowden; J.Mills, K.Elwell, G.Shaw, M.Adams, D.Hull, D.Laughton.
Subs.: W.Ramsey (for Shaw), M.George (for Ramsey).
Referee: Mr. J. Jackson (Pudsey).
Attendance: 16,813. Receipts: £18,677.

1979

Sunday 27th May 1979, at Fartown, Huddersfield.
Leeds 24, Bradford Northern 2.
Leeds: Tries: Alan Smith, David Smith, Ward.
Goals: Dick (7). Drop-goal: Dick.
Bradford: Goal: Ferres.
LEEDS: N.Hague; A.Smith, D.Smith, L.Dyl, J.Atkinson; J.Sanderson, K.Dick; M.Harrison, D.Ward, S.Pitchford, G.Joyce, G.Eccles, P.Cookson.
Subs.: P.Fletcher (for Dyl), B.Adams (for Eccles).
BRADFORD NORTHERN: K.Mumby; D.Parker, E.Okulicz, L.Gant, A.Spencer; S.Ferres, A.Redfearn; J.Thompson, K.Bridges, C.Forsyth, D.Trotter, J.Grayshon, L.Casey. *Subs.: D.Mordue (for Forsyth), I.Van Bellen (for Trotter).*
Referee: Mr. W.H. Thompson (Huddersfield).
Attendance: 19,486. Receipts: £21,291.

THE LEAGUE CHAMPIONS

(*Above*) Featherstone Rovers, the Champions in 1977, and Hull Kingston Rovers, the Champions in 1979.

For most of Rugby League's history its Championship winners had been decided by an end-of-season play-off - traditionally the top-four, and since 1965 a top-16 competition. All that changed when two divisions were introduced in 1973-74 and the league leaders were named as the true Champions. Swinton had claimed this honour in the two years of divisional football in the 'sixties, and it was their neighbours Salford who took the coveted crown in 1973-74. Captained by the Welsh wizard David Watkins, it was ironic that this brilliant Red Devils team of the 'seventies could not achieve such success in the major knockout competitions. But they did repeat their Championship win in 1976 to seal their reputation as one of the teams of the decade. Both Featherstone Rovers and Widnes won the Championship for the first time in their histories in 1977 and 1978. At the same time another race was on to be crowned Second Division Champions, with the prize of promotion accompanied by receipt of the rosebowl trophy.

(*Above*) Salford's David Watkins with the Championship trophy at the end of the 1973-74 season.

FIRST DIVISION

1973-74
Champions: **SALFORD.**
Runners-up: St.Helens.
1974-75
Champions: **ST.HELENS.**
Runners-up: Wigan.
1975-76
Champions: **SALFORD.**
Runners-up: Featherstone.
1976-77
Champions: **FEATHERSTONE.**
Runners-up: St.Helens.
1977-78
Champions: **WIDNES.**
Runners-up: Bradford Northern.
1978-79
Champions: **HULL K.R.**
Runners-up: Warrington.

(*Above*) Tony Miller, captain of Huddersfield, receives the Second Division champions' rosebowl in 1975.

SECOND DIVISION

1973-74
Champions: **BRADFORD N.**
Runners-up: York.
1974-75
Champions: **HUDDERSFIELD.**
Runners-up: Hull K.R.
1975-76
Champions: **BARROW.**
Runners-up: Rochdale Hornets.
1976-77
Champions: **HULL.**
Runners-up: Dewsbury.
1977-78
Champions: **LEIGH.**
Runners-up: Barrow.
1978-79
Champions: **HULL.**
Runner-up: New Hunslet.

LANCASHIRE CUP FINALS

(Above)
Widnes loose-forward Doug Laughton dives over for the late try which snatched the Lancashire Cup from the grasp of holders Workington Town in the 1978 Final at Central Park. Referee Billy Thompson is right on the spot to see the touchdown as Workington stand-off Derek McMillain struggles vainly to hold Laughton back. Other Town players looking on with despair written across their faces are full-back Paul Charlton and hooker Alan Banks. Widnes won 15-13.

The Lancashire Cup Final in the 'seventies did not enjoy the huge attendances which made it such a thrilling event throughout the 1950s, but it still maintained its place as the first major final of each new season and something all the clubs west of the pennines were eager to be a part of. Alex Murphy got the decade off to an exciting start by master-minding Leigh to a narrow win over his old club St.Helens - and this was only the first major trophy of the 1970-71 season for Leigh who went on to taste Wembley glory.

Surprisingly, neither St.Helens nor Warrington (who became one of the game's dominant teams) managed to win the Lancashire Cup during the 'seventies, instead it was Widnes who emerged with a stranglehold on the trophy, winning it five times. And Wigan, who endured one of the least successful decades of their illustrious history during the 1970s, still managed two Lancashire Cup Final wins - the first over Widnes in which they were led by Doug Laughton who would go on to be a major figure in the Chemics' later successes. Doug's finest Lancashire Cup hour came in the 1978 Final against Workington Town on a beautifully sunny October afternoon at Central Park, the typical scenario for a County Cup Final. Widnes had gone three tries down by half-time to the Cumbrian side who were playing in their third consecutive Lancashire Cup Final and displaying a confident style of football befitting of the holders of the trophy. The Chemics seemed to be well beaten as Workington prepared to take the cup with them back to Cumbria, only for Doug Laughton to step up to the plate and drive Widnes forward, Doug himself scoring the late try which edged the Chemics ahead 15-13.

(Left)
Workington Town's joy as they take the Lancashire Cup out of the red rose county for the first time. Town had just beaten Wigan at Wilderspool in the second of their four consecutive Lancashire Cup Finals (1977). In the dressing-room Tom Mitchell proudly holds the Lancashire Cup, alongside fellow Town officials and happy players, led by captain Paul Charlton.

LANCASHIRE CUP FINALS IN THE 'SEVENTIES

1970

Saturday 18 November 1970, at Station Road, Swinton.
Leigh 7, St.Helens 4.
Leigh: Try: Eckersley.
Goals: Ferguson (2).
St.Helens: Goals: Coslett (2).
LEIGH: S.Ferguson; R.Tickle, M.Collins, L.Chisnall, Joe Walsh; D.Eckersley, A.Murphy; D.Chisnall, K.Ashcroft, D.Watts, P.Grimes, G.Clarkson, M.Mooney. *Sub.* T.Canning (for Tickle).
ST.HELENS: F.Barrow; L.Jones, W.Benyon, John Walsh, F.Wilson; F.Myler, A.Whittle; A.Halsall, A.Karalius, G.Rees, J.Mantle, E.Chisnall, K.Coslett. *Sub.* E.Prescott (for Rees).
Referee: Mr. W.H. Thompson (Huddersfield).
Attendance: 10,776. Receipts: £2,735.

1971

Saturday 28 August 1971, at Knowsley Road, St.Helens.
Wigan 15, Widnes 8.
Wigan: Tries: Eastham, Francis, Ayers.
Goals: Tyrer (3).
Widnes: Tries: Gaydon, O'Neill. Goal: Aspey.
WIGAN: C.Tyrer; P.Eastham, W.Francis, C.Fuller, S.Wright; D.Hill, W.Ayers; D.Ashcroft, C.Clarke, G.Fletcher, W.Ashurst, Kevin O'Loughlin, D.Laughton. *Sub.:* D.Gandy (for Wright).
WIDNES: R.Dutton; D.Brown, M.Loughlin, M.Aspey, J.Gaydon; D.O'Neill, R.Bowden; J.Warlow, J.Foran, J.Doughty, J.Kirwan, A.Walsh, G.Nicholls. *Sub.:* G.Lowe (for Walsh).
Referee: Mr. W.H. Thompson (Huddersfield).
Attendance: 6,889. Receipts: £2,204.

1972

Saturday 21 October 1972, at Wilderspool, Warrington.
Salford 25, Swinton 11.
Salford: Tries: Charlton, Eastham, Watkins, Richards, Banner. Goals: Watkins (5).
Swinton: Try: Fleay. Goals: Gowers (3), Kenny.
SALFORD: P.Charlton; P.Eastham, D.Watkins, C.Hesketh, M.Richards; K.Gill, P.Banner; G.Mackay, P.Walker, J.Ward, S.Whitehead, C.Dixon, E.Prescott. *No subs. used.*
SWINTON: P.Jackson; R.Fleay, J.Cooke, A.Buckley, J.Gomersall; P.Kenny, K.Gowers; A.Halsall, R.Evans, H.Bate, R.Smith, G.Hoyle, W.Pattinson. *Subs.:* B.Philbin (for Kenny), W.Holliday (for Bate).
Referee: Mr. W.H. Thompson (Huddersfield).
Attendance: 6,879. Receipts: £3,321.

1973

Saturday 13 October 1973, at Wilderspool, Warrington.
Wigan 19, Salford 9.
Wigan: Tries: O'Loughlin (2), Wright.
Goals: Gray (4), Irving.
Salford: Try: Watkins. Goals: Watkins (3).
WIGAN: W.Francis; G.Vigo, D.Hill, Keiron O'Loughlin, S.Wright; T.Cassidy, W.Ayres; P.Smethurst, C.Clarke, J.Gray, R.Irving, D.Robinson, E.Cunningham. *No subs. used.*
SALFORD: P.Charlton; K.Fielding, D.Watkins, C.Hesketh, I.Holland; K.Gill, P.Banner; G.Mackay, P.Walker, D.Davies, C.Dixon, B.Kear, E.Prescott. *Subs.:* A.Grice (for Davies), J.Knighton (for Kear).
Referee: Mr. W.H. Thompson (Huddersfield).
Attendance: 8,556. Receipts: £3,811.

Salford in the Brian Snape era got their first major silverware by winning the Lancashire Cup in 1972, beating neighbours Swinton in the final. But, remarkably, the Red Devils failed to repeat that win, finishing runners-up in the next three Lancashire Cup Finals. That 1972 final at Wilderspool was the first one to be sponsored - and it caused some discussion that the title sponsors were Tetleys, a brewery more associated with Yorkshire, rather than Lancashire. They had to explain that they had a major west of the pennines base at Warrington brewery.

(Left)
Salford's centre Chris Hesketh tangles with Widnes winger Alan Prescott as the ball goes loose in the 1975 Lancashire Cup Final at Wigan.

1974

Saturday 2nd November 1974, at Central Park, Wigan.
Widnes 6, Salford 2.
Widnes: Try: George.
Goal: Dutton. Drop-goal: Hughes.
Salford: Goal: Fielding.
WIDNES: R.Dutton; M.George, D.O'Neill, M.Aspey, A.Prescott; E.Hughes, R.Bowden; J.Mills, K.Elwell, J.Stephens, M.Adams, R.Blackwood, D.Laughton. *No subs. used.*
SALFORD: P.Charlton; K.Fielding, C.Dixon, G.Graham, M.Richards; J.Taylor, P.Banner; G.Mackay, E.Devlin, A.Grice, J.Knighton, M.Coulman, E.Prescott. *No subs. used.*
Referee: Mr. G.F. Lindop (Wakefield).
Attendance: 6,703. Receipts: £2,832.

1975

Saturday 4th October 1975, at Central Park, Wigan.
Widnes 16, Salford 7.
Widnes: Tries: Prescott, George, Aspey.
Goals: Dutton (3).
Drop-goal: Dutton.
Salford: Try: Richards. Goals: Watkins (2).
WIDNES: R.Dutton; A.Prescott, M.George, M.Aspey, D.Jenkins; E.Hughes, R.Bowden; J.Mills, K.Elwell, N.Nelson, J.Foran, J.Fitzpatrick, M.Adams. *Sub. B.Sheridan (for Fitzpatrick).*
SALFORD: D.Watkins; K.Fielding, J.Butler, C.Hesketh, M.Richards; K.Gill, S.Nash; J.Fiddler, R.Hawksley, C.Dixon, S.Turnbull, J. Knighton, E.Prescott. *Sub.: G.Mackay (for Dixon).*
Referee: Mr. W.H. Thompson (Huddersfield).
Attendance: 7,266. Receipts: £3,880.

1976

Saturday 30th October 1976, at Central Park, Wigan.
Widnes 16, Workington Town 11.
Widnes: Tries: Wright, George.
Goals: Dutton (4). Drop-goals: Dutton, Bowden.
Workington: Try: Wilkins. Goals: MacCorquodale (4).
WIDNES: R.Dutton; S.Wright, M.Aspey, M.George, A.Prescott; D.Eckersley, R.Bowden; W.Ramsey, K.Elwell, N.Nelson, A.Dearden, M.Adams, D.Laughton. *No subs. used.*
WORKINGTON TOWN: P.Charlton; D.Collister, R.Wilkins, I.Wright, I.MacCorquodale; B.Lauder, A.Walker; J.Mills, A.Banks, R.Calvin, E.Bowman, L.Gorley, W.Pattinson. *Sub.: P.Gorley (for Pattinson).*
Referee: Mr. W.H. Thompson (Huddersfield).
Attendance: 9,399. Receipts: £6,414.

1977

Saturday 29 October 1977, at Wilderspool, Warrington.
Workington Town 16, Wigan 13.
Workington: Tries: Wright, Wilkins.
Goals: MacCorquodale (4). Drop-goals: Walker (2).
Wigan: Tries: Nulty, Ashurst, Willicombe.
Goals: Nulty, Burke.
WORKINGTON TOWN: P.Charlton; D.Collister, J.Risman, I.Wright, I.MacCorquodale; R.Wilkins, A.Walker; D.Watts, A.Banks, E.Bowman, L.Gorley, P.Gorley, W.Pattinson. *Sub.: D.Atkinson (for Charlton).*
WIGAN: M.Swann; G.Vigo, D.Willicombe, S.Davies, J.Hornby; A.Taylor, J.Nulty; B.Hogan, G.Aspinall, R.Irving, W.Melling, W.Ashurst, R.Blackwood. *Subs.: J.Burke (for Davies), D.Regan (for Melling)*
Referee: Mr. W.H. Thompson (Huddersfield).
Attendance: 9,548. Receipts: £5,038.

Sponsorship branding had changed to become the Forshaws Lancashire Cup by the mid-1970s, backed by the Burtonwood brewery of Warrington, and throughout this era Workington Town's passion for the competition knew no bounds. Winning the Lancashire Cup had become like the quest for the Holy Grail by Town's charismatic leader Tom Mitchell, and he finally got his wish in 1977 when Wigan were beaten 16-13 in a rip-roaring final. Workington followed this by coming so close to retaining the cup against Widnes the following year. Alas, by the time their fourth consecutive final came arouund in 1979, Workington's great side had started to break up - they even found one of their favourites, Les Gorley, playing on the opposing side for the ultimate winners, Widnes.

(Above) **The maestro at work as Alex Murphy plotted the downfall of his old club Saints in the 1970 Lancashire Cup Final at Swinton. Murphy guided Leigh to a 7-4 victory and a first major trophy in a season which ended with them winning the Challenge Cup at Wembley. In this picture, Alex puts in one of his astute kicks watched by stand-off David Eckersley and the St.Helens loose-forward Kel Coslett. This was one trophy the Saints could not get their hands on during the 'seventies.**

(Above) **Workington Town chairman George Graham and coach Ike Southward lead their team out, headed by captain Paul Charlton, alongside the Wigan side with Brian Hogan first on the picture, before the 1977 Lancashire Cup Final at Wilderspool. It proved to be a momentous day in the history of the Town club.**

1978

Saturday 7th October 1978, at Central Park, Wigan.
Widnes 15, Workington Town 13.
Widnes: Tries: Laughton (2), Wright. Goals: Burke (3).
Workington: Tries: Wilkins, MacCorquodale, L.Gorley.
Goals: MacCorquodale (2).
WIDNES: D.Eckersley; S.Wright, M.Aspey, M.George, M.Burke; E.Hughes, R.Bowden; J.Mills, K.Elwell, G.Shaw, M.Adams, A.Dearden, D.Laughton. *Sub.:* D.Hull (for Dearden).
WORKINGTON TOWN: P.Charlton; D.Collister, J.Risman, R.Wilkins, I.MacCorquodale; D.McMillan, A.Walker; H.Beverley, A.Banks, E.Bowman, P.Gorley, R.Blackwood, W.Pattinson.
Sub.: L.Gorley (for Pattinson).
Referee: Mr. W.H. Thompson (Huddersfield).
Attendance: 10,020. Receipts: £9,936.

1979

Saturday 8th December 1979, at The Willows, Salford.
Widnes 11, Workington Town 0.
Widnes: Tries: Moran, Adams.
Goals: Burke (2).
Drop-goal: Elwell.
WIDNES: D.Eckersley; S.Wright, M.Aspey, E.Hughes, M.Burke; D.Moran, R.Bowden; B.Hogan, K.Elwell, G.Shaw, L.Gorley, A.Dearden, M.Adams.
Sub.: M.George (for Hughes).
WORKINGTON TOWN: P.Charlton; I.MacCorquodale, K.Maughan, I.Thompson, D.Beck; I.Rudd, A.Walker; H.Beverley, A.Banks, G.Wallbanks, W.Pattinson, R.Lewis, J.Dobie.
Subs.: T.Roper (for Walker), A.Varty (for Wallbanks).
Referee: Mr. W.H. Thompson (Huddersfield).
Attendance: 6,887. Receipts: £7,100.

YORKSHIRE CUP FINALS

I t was ironic that it was the Yorkshire Cup, probably the most traditional old competition in Rugby League, which found itself most embroiled in controversies and new innovations as the game struggled to adapt to the changing attitudes of the 'seventies. The decade started badly when Hunslet were unable to take part in the 1970 competition because their players were on strike, and worse was to come the following year when the Yorkshire Cup gave a trial run to summer rugby, kicking off at the end of July and playing through the early weeks of August. Leeds thought it ridiculous that the season should be starting in July and promptly stated they would withdraw from the Yorkshire Cup – this led to them being banned from the following year's tournament (a ban which was later to be rescinded). So, the 1971 competition kicked off without Leeds and also Dewsbury who, with such an early start, had been unable to agree terms with their players for the new season. The Yorkshire County secretary, Mr. W.H. "George" Hirst, believed it was too hot to be playing cup ties in early August and suggested they should be played in four quarters with intervals of three minutes for drinks. In the event, the idea of summer rugby was given a strong thumbs-down when a total attendance of only 14,000 could be mustered for all the first round games.

(Above)
Leeds celebrate with the Yorkshire Cup in 1975. The players are, left to right: Eccles, Marshall, Dickinson, Smith, Hynes, Dyl, Harrison and Hepworth.

The experiment of such an early start to the season was because of the perceived demands later in the year of a brand new sponsored knockout tournament being introduced to Rugby League, which turned out to be the Players No.6 Trophy; plus there was a desire to avoid clashes with the New Zealanders' tour to this country. In the event, Hull Kingston Rovers beat Castleford to win the 1971 Yorkshire Cup Final which was played on 21st August, some two months earlier than the usual date, at Wakefield's Belle Vue ground.

Sponsorship arrived for the Yorkshire Cup in 1972 when Esso Petroleum pumped (!) £2,500 into the tournament. Branded as the Esso Yorkshire Cup, the sponsorship money rose to £6,000 the following year and had risen to £9,000 by 1978 when the Yorkshire County R.L. also had additional sponsorship support from Rowntree Mackintosh (the chocolate makers.) But the sponsorship did come at an uncomfortable price when, after dipping their toes successfully in the water, Esso's marketing people decided that all future Yorkshire Cup Finals under their branding had to be played at Headingley.

(Above) **Barry Banks - starred for York in the 1978 final.**

(Above)
Sponsorship arrived in the Yorkshire Cup from Esso.

Rugby League Football

The Esso Yorkshire County Challenge Cup

Yorkshire Rugby at its best

There's a game around your way so follow your team, they could be winners!

You're in good company with **Esso**

This was because they believed Headingley was the only venue among the Yorkshire grounds with the off-field facilities good enough to stage such a prestigious event. It was a time honoured tradition that County Cup finals should be played on neutral grounds and the decision to make Headingley the venue, even if the host club Leeds were involved, did not go down well with the other clubs and their supporters. And the Loiners certainly went on to make that home advantage pay, winning four Yorkshire Cup Finals on home soil later in the decade, but not before they added another in 1972 at Odsal Stadium where they walloped Dewsbury 36-9. Few could have predicted that Dewsbury would take such a spectacular revenge later that season at the very same venue.

(Right) **Dewsbury prop Dick "Trevor" Lowe on the attack against Leeds in the 1972 Yorkshire Cup Final at Odsal.**

Yorkshire Cup Finals in the 'Seventies

1970
Saturday 21 November 1970, at Odsal Stad., Bradford.
Leeds 23, Featherstone Rovers 7.
Leeds: Tries: Smith (2), Atkinson, Dunn, Ramsey.
Goals: Hynes (4).
Featherstone: Try: Hartley. **Goals:** Kellett (2).
LEEDS: J.Holmes; A.Smith, S.Hynes, R.Cowan, J.Atkinson; A.Wainwright, M.Shoebottom; J.Burke, P.Dunn, P.Cookson, W.Ramsey, R.Haigh, R.Batten.
Sub.: J.Langley (for Wainwright).
FEATHERSTONE ROVERS: C.Kellett; M.Smith, K.Cotton, J.Newlove, D.Hartley; C.Harding, T.Hudson; D.Windmill, D.Morgan, S.Lyons, A.Rhodes, J.Thompson, V.Farrar.
Sub.: P.Coventry (for Harding).
Referee: Mr. D.S. Brown (Preston).
Attendance: 6,533. **Receipts:** £1,879.

1971
Saturday 21st August 1971, at Belle Vue, Wakefield.
Hull K.R. 11, Castleford 7.
Hull K.R.: Try: Longstaffe. **Goals:** Millward (4).
Castleford: Try: Foster. **Goals:** Ackroyd (2).
HULL K.R.: I.Markham; M.Stephenson, P.Coupland, G.Kirkpatrick, P.Longstaffe; R.Millward, P.Daley; S.Wiley, P.Flanagan, J.Millington, C.Wallis, E.Palmer, J.Brown.
Sub.: C.Cooper (for Palmer).
CASTLEFORD: D.Edwards; D.Foster, S.Norton, K.Worsley, A.Lowndes; D.Hargrave, G.Stephens; D.Hartley, A.Miller, I.Van Bellen, B.Lockwood, A.Dickinson, G.Blakeway.
Sub.: A.Ackroyd (for Van Bellen).
Referee: Mr. A. Givvons (Oldham).
Attendance: 5,536. **Receipts:** £1,589.

1972
Saturday 7th October 1972, at Odsal Stadium, Bradford.
Leeds 36, Dewsbury 9.
Leeds: Tries: Holmes (3), Dyl (2), Atkinson, Hardisty, Eccles.
Goals: Clawson (5), Hynes.
Dewsbury: Try: Ashcroft. **Goals:** Agar (3).
LEEDS: J.Holmes; A.Smith, S.Hynes, L.Dyl, J.Atkinson; A.Hardisty, K.Hepworth; T.Clawson, D.Ward, W.Ramsey, P.Cookson, G.Eccles, R.Batten.
Subs.: J.Langley (for Hepworth), A.Fisher (for Clawson).
DEWSBURY: A.Rushton; G.Ashcroft, A.Childs, T.Day, J.Yoward; A.Agar, A.Bates; G.Bell, M.Stephenson, T.Lowe, J.Grayshon, J.Bates, S.Hankins.
Subs.: S.Lee (for J.Bates), H.Beverley (for Bell).
Referee: Mr. M.J. Naughton (Widnes).
Attendance: 7,406. **Receipts:** £2,659.

1973
Saturday 20th October 1973, at Headingley, Leeds.
Leeds 7, Wakefield Trinity 2.
Leeds: Try: Langley. **Goals:** Hynes, Marshall.
Wakefield: Goal: Crook.
LEEDS: J.Holmes; J.Langley, S.Hynes, L.Dyl, J.Atkinson; A.Hardisty, K.Hepworth; D.Jeanes, D.Ward, G.Clarkson, P.Cookson, G.Eccles, R.Batten.
Subs.: D.Marshall (for Langley), W.Ramsey (for Jeanes).
WAKEFIELD TRINITY: G.Wraith; D.Smith, T.Crook, J.Hegarty, B.Parker; D.Topliss, J.Bonnar; R.Valentine, M.Morgan, R.Bratt, D.Knowles, K.Endersby, E.Holmes. *Subs.:* L.Sheard (for Wraith), G.Ballantyne (for Knowles).
Referee: Mr. M.J.Naughton (Widnes).
Attendance: 7,621. **Receipts:** £4,100.

(Above, left)
Joe Brown, the Hull K.R. loose-forward, on the attack against Wakefield in the 1974 Final.
(Above, right)
David Smith and Les Dyl defend for Leeds against Featherstone in the 1976 Final.

The first of those four Leeds Yorkshire Cup Final home ground triumphs was a 7-2 win over Wakefield in 1973, and they all proved to be very close encounters with relatively low scorelines. Leeds at Headingley were always favourites to win, and with such quality international players in their back division like: John Holmes, Alan Smith, Les Dyl, Syd Hynes and John Atkinson, the Loiners rarely disappointed, despite the brave fforts of opponents Hull K.R., Featherstone Rovers and Halifax, in addition to the aforementioned Wakefield Trinity. The famous cup fighters of Featherstone, not content with going to Wembley twice in a row, were unlucky to go down twice in consecutive Yorkshire Cup Finals, in 1976 and '77.

1974
Saturday 26th October 1974, at Headingley, Leeds.
Hull K.R. 16, Wakefield Trinity 13.
Hull K.R.: Tries: Watson (2), Kirkpatrick, Dunn.
Goals: Fox (2).
Wakefield: Tries: Smith, Hegarty, Bratt.
Goals: Crook (2).
HULL K.R.: R.Smithies; C.Sullivan, B.Watson, P.Coupland, G.Kirkpatrick; R.Millward, M.Stephenson; J.Millington, I.Heslop, P.Rose, C.Wallis, N.Fox, J.Brown.
Subs.: G.Dunn (for Sullivan), I.Madley (for Fox).
WAKEFIELD TRINITY: L.Sheard; D.Smith, T.Crook, J.Hegarty, J.Archer; D.Topliss, J.Bonnar; G.Ballantyne, R.Handscombe, R.Bratt, T.Skerrett, A.Tonks, M.Morgan. *Subs.:* N.Goodwin (forTonks), E.Holmes (for Goodwin).
Referee: Mr. M.J. Naughton (Widnes).
Attendance: 5,639. Receipts: £3,337.

1975
Saturday 15th November 1975, at Headingley, Leeds.
Leeds 15, Hull K.R. 11.
Leeds: Tries: Dyl, Cookson.
Goals: Holmes (4). Drop-goal: Holmes.
Hull K.R.: Tries: Sullivan, Fox.
Goals:: Fox (2). Drop-goal: Millward.
LEEDS: D.Marshall; A.Smith, N.Hague, L.Dyl, J.Atkinson; J.Holmes, S.Hynes; M.Harrison, I.Payne, S.Pitchford, G.Eccles, R.Batten, P.Cookson.
Sub.: R.Dickinson (for Pitchford).

HULL K.R. R.Wallace; G.Dunn, A.Burwell, B.Watson, C.Sullivan; G.Turner, R.Millward; J.Millington, C.Dickinson, S.Lyons, P.Rose, N.Fox, M.Hughes. *Sub.:* R.Holdstock (for Hughes).
Referee: Mr. J.V. Moss (Manchester).
Attendance: 5,305.
Receipts: £3,906.

(Above)
John Millington, the Hull K.R. prop played in three Yorkshire Cup Finals in the 'seventies.

1976
Saturday 16th October 1976, at Headingley, Leeds.
Leeds 16, Featherstone Rovers 12.
Leeds: Tries: Dyl (2), Eccles, Cookson.
Goals: Marshall (2).
Featherstone: Tries: Bray, Smith.
Goals: Quinn (3).
LEEDS: D.Marshall; N.Hague, S.Hynes, L.Dyl, D.Smith; J.Holmes, P.Banner; R.Dickinson, D.Ward, S.Pitchford, G.Eccles, C.Burton, P.Cookson.
FEATHERSTONE ROVERS: H.Box; G.Bray, P.Coventry, S.Quinn, K.Kellett; J.Newlove, D.Fennell; M.Gibbins, K.Bridges, V.Farrar, R.Stone, P.Smith, K.Bell. *Sub.:* J.A.Spells (for Bell).
Referee: Mr. M.J. Naughton (Widnes).
Attendance: 7,644. Receipts: £5,197.

The game's legendary points scorer Neil Fox - a veteran of several previous Yorkshire Cup Finals with Wakefield - played in two finals for Hull K.R. in the 'seventies and then in a third in 1978 for Bradford Northern as they beat gallant York in the best supported final of the decade. York's appearance in the final as a Second Division club, showed just how much of an incentive the County Cups were for the so-called "smaller" clubs, and that lesson was learned again the following year when Halifax, also in the Second Division, made it through to the final. Coached by Maurice Bamford, they put up a mighty struggle against Leeds and showed the form that would take them to a Challenge Cup semi-final later that season. No club enjoyed winning the Yorkshire Cup in the 1970s more than Castleford - a club with Wembley victories behind them, and stars of the modern era, Malcolm Reilly became the very first Cas' captain to lift the old trophy when his team finally won it in 1977.

(Above)
Malcolm Reilly, the Castelford player-coach, displays the Yorkshire Cup in 1977.

(Above)
Halifax loose-forward Dave Busfield looks about to be crunched by the Leeds props Roy Dickinson and Steve Pitchford as 'Fax went down bravely in the 1979 Yorkshire Cup Final.

1977

Saturday 15th October 1977, at Headingley, Leeds.

Castleford 17, Featherstone Rovers 7.

Castleford: Tries: Burton (2).
Goals: Lloyd (5). Drop-goal: Burton.
Featherstone: Try: Smith. Goals: Quinn, Townend.
CASTLEFORD: G.Wraith; T.Richardson, J.Joyner, P.Johnson, S.Fenton; B.Burton, C.Pickerill; A.Fisher, R.Spurr, A.Weston, J.Huddleston, M.Reilly, G.Lloyd. *Subs.:* G.Stephens (for Pickerill). D.Woodall (for Fisher).
FEATHERSTONE ROVERS: J.Marsden; S.Evans, J.Gilbert, S.Quinn, K.Kellett; J.Newlove, P.Butler; J.Townend, K.Bridges, V.Farrar, M.Gibbins, R.Stone, K.Bell. *Subs.:* N.Tuffs (for Quinn), P.Smith (for Stone).
Referee: Mr. M.J. Naughton (Widnes).
Attendance: 6,318. Receipts: £4,528.

1978

Saturday 28th October 1978, at Headingley, Leeds.

Bradford Northern 18, York 8.

Bradford: Tries: Gant, Parker, Alan Redfearn, Haigh.
Goals: Fox (3).
York: Try: Smith. Goals: Banks (2). Drop-goal: Hollis.
BRADFORD NORTHERN: K.Mumby; D.Barends, L.Gant, D.Parker, D.Redfearn; I.Slater, D.Redfearn; J.Thompson, A.Fisher, C.Forsyth, N.Fox, D.Trotter, R.Haigh. *Subs.:* J.Wolford (for Slater), G.Joyce (for Forsyth).

YORK: G.Smith; T.Morgan, T.Day, D.Foster, G.Nicholson; B.Banks, K.Harkin; D.Dunkerley, R.Wileman, W.Harris, A.Rhodes, B.Hollis, S.Cooper.
Subs.: J.Crossley (for Day), T.Ramshaw (for Hollis).
Referee: Mr. M.J. Naughton (Widnes).
Attendance: 10,429.
Receipts: £9,188.

(Above) Graham Joyce, subbed for Bradford Northern in the 1978 Final.

1979

Saturday 27th Otober 1979, at Headingley, Leeds.

Leeds 15, Halifax 6.

Leeds: Tries: Alan Smith (2), David Smith.
Goals: Dick (3).
Halifax: Goals: Birts (3).
LEEDS: N.Hague; A.Smith, D.Smith, L.Dyl, J.Atkinson; J.Holmes, K.Dick; R.Dickinson, D.Ward, S.Pitchford, G.Eccles, D.Heron, P.Cookson. *Subs.:* J.Sanderson (for Holmes), B.Adams (for Heron).
HALIFAX: J.Birts; D.Howard, G.Garrod, D.Cholmondley, K.Waites; M.Blacker, T.Langton; P.Jarvis, D.Raistrick, A.Wood, M.Scott, G.Sharp, D.Busfield. *Subs.:* M.Snee (for Howard), D.Callon (for Jarvis).
Referee: Mr. M.J. Naughton (Widnes).
Attendance: 9,134. Receipts: £9,999.

PLAYERS TROPHY FINALS

(*Above*) **A famous try in the second Players No. 6 Trophy Final in 1973 as Leeds winger John Atkinson outpaces Salford prop Terry Ramshaw to claim one his two touchdowns in the Loiners' 12-7 victory at Fartown.**

PLAYER'S Nº6 TROPHY FINAL

OFFICIAL PROGRAMME   PRICE 10p

Rugby League's first major sponsored competition was introduced in the 1971-72 season with the launch of the Players No. 6 Trophy. It came as the fruition of an association between the game and the John Player and Sons company which had begun in 1967 with the introduction of the Players No. 6 player-of-the-match awards. In 1971-72 a knockout tournament (on the same lines as the Challenge Cup) was introduced involving the 30 senior clubs and two leading amateur teams. With prize money of £5,000 for the winners on offer, and a chance to stage an additional big event televised live on the BBC, the Final of the Players No. 6 Trophy quickly became a major attraction.

Halifax wrote their name into the game's history as the very first winners of the new competition, beating Wakefield Trinity 22-11 in the inaugural final played at Odsal Stadium. Halifax had shown their cup fighting qualities by beating both Warrington and Leeds away on their way to that first final, and then coming back from a half-time deficit to overcome Wakefield. Thus Gordon Baker became the first captain to lift the new trophy, with Halifax's regular captain Derek Reeves on the substitutes' bench. The man-of-the-match award in the first Players No. 6 Trophy final went to stand-off Bruce Burton, whose accurate kicking scored ten points.

The new tournament quickly came of age in its second campaign when the glamour teams from rival sides of the Pennines, Salford and Leeds, met in the Final at Huddersfield. Salford were pre-match favourites to win a £100 bonus plus a three-day holiday in Majorca, but it was Leeds who prevailed - guided by the former Castleford half-back pair of Hardisty and Hepworth in a final which featured a spectacular one handed 'American Football style' pass by John Holmes which put John Atkinson in for a try at the corner. By its third season in 1973-74, the Players No. 6 Trophy had established its reputation for giving some of the less fashionable clubs a taste of the big time as Rochdale Hornets helped put on an entertaining final with Warrington.

(Right) **Halifax captain Gordon Baker was the first man to receive the Players No. 6 Trophy after leading his team to victory over Wakefield Trinity in the inaugral final, played at Odsal Stadium in 1972.**

PLAYERS TROPHY FINALS IN THE 'SEVENTIES

1972

Saturday 22 January 1972, at Odsal Stadium, Bradford.
Halifax 22, Wakefield Trinity 11.
Halifax: Tries: Davies, Willicombe, Kelly, Callon.
Goals: Burton (5).
Wakefield: Tries: Marston, Topliss, Valentine.
Goal: Fox.
HALIFAX: A.Hepworth; D.Raynor, P.Davies, D.Willicombe, M.Kelly; B.Burton, G.Baker; T.Dewhirst, R.Hawksley, D.Callon, T.Fogerty, J.Martin, T.Halmshaw. *Subs.: J.Sanderson (for Baker), D.Reeves (for Callon).*
WAKEFIELD TRINITY: G.Wraith; K.Slater, J.Marston, J.Hegarty, M.Major; D.Topliss, K.Harkin; D.Jeanes, M.Morgan, S.Lyons, P.Harrison, R.Valentine, N.Fox. *Subs.: B.Ward (for Wraith), R.Spencer (for Harrison).*
Referee: Mr. S. Shepherd (Oldham).
Attendance: 7,975. Receipts: £2,545.

1973

Saturday 24th March 1973, at Fartown, Huddersfield.
Leeds 12, Salford 7.
Leeds: Tries: Atkinson (2).
Goals: Clawson (2), Holmes.
Salford: Try: Dixon. Goals: Watkins (2).
LEEDS: J.Holmes; A.Smith, S.Hynes, L.Dyl, J.Atkinson; A.Hardisty, K.Hepworth; T.Clawson, A.Fisher, D.Jeanes. R.Haigh, P.Cookson, G.Eccles. *Subs.: P.Pickup (for Fisher), D.Ward (for Clawson).*
SALFORD: P.Charlton; T.Colloby, D.Watkins, C.Hesketh, M.Richards; K.Gill, P.Banner; T.Ramshaw, J.Ward, G.Mackay, A.Grice, W.Kirkbride, C.Dixon.
Subs.: P.Ward (for Gill), D.Davies (for Grice).
Referee: Mr. W.H. Thompson (Huddersfield).
Attendance: 10,102. Receipts: £4,563.

1974

Saturday 9th February 1974, at Central Park, Wigan.
Warrington 27, Rochdale Hornets 16.
Warrington: Tries: Noonan (2), Whitehead, Bevan, Nicholas.
Goals: Whitehead (6).
Rochdale: Tries: Brelsford (2), Brophy, Taylor.
Goals: Holliday (2).
WARRINGTON: D.Whitehead; M.Philbin, D.Noonan, F.Reynolds, J.Bevan; A.Whittle, P.Gordon; D.Chisnall, K.Ashcroft, B.Brady, D.Wright, R.Wanbon, B.Philbin. *Subs.: W.Pickup (for Reynolds), M.Nicholas (for Chisnall).*
ROCHDALE HORNETS: J.Crellin; N.Brelsford, T.Brophy, D.Taylor, W.Aspinall; J.Butler, P.Gartland; W.Holliday, R.Harris, S.Whitehead, T.Fogerty, W.Sheffield, T.Halmshaw.
Sub.: H.Wood (for Fogerty).
Referee: Mr. G. Kershaw (York).
Attendance: 9,347. Receipts: £4,380.

1975

Saturday 25 January 1975, at Wilderspool, Warrington.
Bradford Northern 3, Widnes 2.
Bradford: Try: Carlton.
Widnes: Goal: Dutton.
BRADFORD NORTHERN: S.Carlton; R.Francis, P.Ward, L.Gant, D.Redfearn; M.Blacker, B.Seabourne; K.Earl, F.Jarvis, P.Jackson, G.Joyce, D.Trotter, S.Fearnley.
WIDNES: R.Dutton; A.Prescott, D.O'Neill, M.Aspey, C.Anderson; E.Hughes, R.Bowden; J.Mills, K.Elwell, B.Sheridan, M.Adams, R.Blackwood, D.Laughton.
Referee: Mr. G.F. Lindop (Wakefield).
Attendance: 5,935. Receipts: £3,305.

(Above)
Action from the 1975 Players No. 6 Trophy Final at Wilderspool, as Widnes prop Jim Mills ploughs through the Bradford Northern defence. Big Jim played in three Players Trophy Finals in the 'seventies and 1975 was the only losing one.

(Above, right)
Bradford loose-forward Stan Fearnley celebrates with champagne over the head of full-back Stuart Carlton, who scored the only try of the 1975 Final as Northern won 3-2.

(Above) Castleford scrum-half Gary Stephens sprints for the line to score a try in 1977 Final against Blackpool Borough at The Willows; Blackpool winger Phil Pitman gives chase as referee Mick Naughton looks on. The class and pace of Cas' told in the end, but "little" Blackpool, in their first major final, won many friends with a magnificent effort.

1976
Saturday 24th January 1976, at Headingley, Leeds.
Widnes 19, Hull 13.
Widnes: Tries: *Jenkins (2), Bowden, Adams.*
Goals: *Dutton (3).*
Drop-goal: *Bowden.*
Hull: Tries: *Crane (2), Hunter.*
Goals: *Boxall (2).*
WIDNES: R.Dutton; A.Prescott, M.George, M.Aspey, D.Jenkins; E.Hughes, R.Bowden; J.Mills, K.Elwell, J.Wood, J.Foran, B.Sheridan, M.Adams.
HULL: M.Stephenson; A.Macklin, G.Clark, S.Portz, P.Hunter; B.Hancock, K.Foulkes; W.Ramsey, P.Flanagan, A.Wardell, K.Boxall, M.Walker, M.Crane. *Sub.:* C.Davidson (for Foulkes).
Referee: Mr. J. V. Moss (Manchester).
Attendance: 9,035. *Receipts:* £6,275.

1977
Saturday 22nd January 1977, at The Willows, Salford.
Castleford 25, Blackpool Borough 15.
Castleford: Tries: *Wraith, Joyner, Johnson, Burton, Stephens.* **Goals:** *Lloyd (5).*
Blackpool: Tries: *Allen, Egan, Machen.*
Goals: *Egan (3).*
CASTLEFORD: G.Wraith; S.Fenton, J.Joyner, P.Johnson, T.Briggs; B.Burton, G.Stephens; P.Khan, R.Spurr, A.Dickinson, M.Reilly, G.Lloyd, S.Norton.
BLACKPOOL BOROUGH: D.Reynolds; D.Robinson, J.Heritage, P.Machen, P.Pitman; G.Marsh, J.Newall; J.Hamilton, H.Allen, J.Egan, P.Gamble, K.Groves, M.Pattinson.
Subs.: C.Lamb (for Pitman), P.Hurst (for Groves).
Referee: Mr. M.J. Naughton (Widnes).
Attendance: 4,512. *Receipts:* £2,919.

As a precursor to Blackpool Borough's memorable appearance in the 1977 final, Hull had also belied their Second Division status to qualify for the 1976 final in which they gave favourites Widnes a real run for their money at Headingley, with loose-forward Mick Crane scoring two tries.

A feature of all the finals was the presentation of a silver salver to the man-of-the-match, and the 1974 winner - Warrington hooker Kevin Ashcroft *(pictured, left, with scrum-half Parry Gordon)* - made the grand gesture of presenting his £25 prize money to the Wigan groundsman Billy Mitchell, who had done a fine job in getting the rain-soaked Central Park pitch fit for play.

Well established as the game's biggest sponsored tournament by the end of the decade, a new name of 'The John Player Competition' replaced the original Players No. 6 Trophy tag in the 1977-78 season.

(Above) **Widnes captain Reg Bowden is presented with the John Player Trophy after the Chemics had beaten Warrington in the 1979 Final at Knowsley Road, St.Helens. The Rugby Football League secretary, David Oxley, is ready to present the winners with their medals. It was a revenge win for Widnes over their local rivals, after they had lost to Warrington in the 1978 Final.**

1978

Saturday 28 January 1978, at Knowsley Rd. St.Helens.
Warrington 9, Widnes 4.
Warrington: Try: Bevan. Goals: Hesford (3).
Widnes: Goals: Woods (2).
WARRINGTON: D.Finnigan; S.Hesford, W.Benyon, F.Wilson, J.Bevan; K.Kelly, P.Gordon; R.Lester, J.Dalgreen, M.Nicholas, T.Martyn, B.Philbin, I.Potter.
WIDNES: D.Eckersley; S.Wright, M.Aspey, M.George, P.Woods; E.Hughes, R.Bowden; W.Ramsey, K.Elwell, G.Shaw, M.Adams, D.Hull, D.Laughton. *Sub.:* A.Dearden (for Shaw).
Referee: Mr. W.H. Thompson (Huddersfield).
Attendance: 10,258. Receipts: £8,429.

1979

Saturday 28th April 1979, at Knowsley Raod, St.Helens.
Widnes 28, Warrington 4.
Widnes: Tries: Wright, Hull. Goals: Burke (3).
Drop-goals: Elwell (2), Adams (2).
Warrington: Goals: Hesford (2).
WIDNES: D.Eckersley; S.Wright, E.Hughes, M.Aspey, M.Burke; D.Moran, R.Bowden; J.Mills, K.Elwell, G.Shaw, A.Dearden, D.Hull, M.Adams.
WARRINGTON: D.Finnigan; M.Kelly, S.Hesford, W.Benyon, D.Sutton; K.Kelly, P.,Gordon; R.Lester, A.Walker, M.Nicholas, B.Case, T.Martyn, A.Gwilliam. *Sub.:* E.Hunter (for Kelly).
Referee: Mr. G.F. Lindop (Wakefield).
Attendance: 10,743. Receipts: £11,710.

FLOODLIT TROPHY FINALS

Programme from the first BBC Floodlit Trophy Final of the 1970/71 season.

B.B.C.2 TV
FLOODLIT COMPETITION FINAL
LEEDS v. ST.HELENS
on Tuesday 15th December 1970
at Headingley Grounds Leeds
Kick-off 7-15 p.m.

OFFICIAL PROGRAMME 6d.

The seeds for the BBC 2 Television Floodlit Competition were sown in early 1965 following the broadcast on the BBC's *"Sportsnight"* programme of the St.Helens versus Other Nationalities match played to mark the switch-on of the new floodlights at Knowsley Road. At that time, only three clubs: Leigh, Swinton and St.Helens, had operational floodlights with Castleford nearing completion of their's - most clubs being reluctant to invest their money on this venture after finding that one of the early pioneers of floodlighting, Leigh, constantly had difficulty in persuading other clubs to play under lights in their belief that it gave the home club an advantage.

But when the BBC launched their Channel 2 in the north of England in October 1965 they were eager to test outside broadcasts, and offered to televise a floodlit Rugby League competition in mid-week, thus providing viewers with a choice of entertainment and a complete contrast to their normal programming. It was an instant success and the message quickly spread among Rugby League clubs that it paid to have lights, as the BBC competition was offering prize money which would enable clubs to profit from their investment. Very quickly the following clubs were "lit up": Barrow, Leeds, Wigan, Hull K.R., Halifax, Salford, Huddersfield, Keighley, Warrington, Widnes, Hull, Oldham and Rochdale Hornets. Others followed suit as the BBC 2 Floodlit competition became such a popular feature on the fixture list and also provided the Rugby League game with such wonderful publicity by having national television coverage at prime time on Tuesday evenings.

The Rugby League also used the Floodlit competition to give a trial run of the four-tackle rule which they rapidly introduced to the game as a whole in the autumn of 1966. Castleford were the club who profited most in the

(Above)
Programme from the first BBC Floodlit Trophy Final of the 1970s - Leeds versus St.Helens.

(Above)
The BBC's head of outside broadcasts, Cliff Morgan, always a fan of Rugby League, presents the Floodlit Trophy to Castleford's Malcolm Reilly in 1976.

early years of the Floodlit Trophy, winning it for the first three years and bathing in the glory of being a "glamour" club regularly featured on television. By the time the 'seventies came around "Tuesday night floodlit rugby" was a massive drawcard for the game every season as autumn turned to winter. The final each year, played on a Tuesday night in December not long before Christmas, attracted prestigious guests from the BBC hierachy, and became a major target for all the top clubs - not that they had it all their own way and several of the less fashionable sides, including Dewsbury, Rochdale Hornets and Bramley enjoyed their moments in the t.v. spotlight. No triumph was more joyous, and more appreciated throughout the game as a whole, than Bramley's in 1973. It brought "The Villagers" their first ever major trophy and, in rather bizarre circumstances, saw a floodlit competition being played in daylight. Because of restrictions on the use of electricity due to a power shortage, Bramley had to play both their semi-final win over St.Helens at McLaren Field, and then the final away at Naughton Park in Widnes, during daylight hours on Tuesday afternoons, with the games being broadcast in the evening.

Bramley's moment of glory

(Above) Bramley's Trevor Briggs is tackled by Widnes hooker Keith Elwell in the 1973 Floodlit Trophy Final. Bramley winning the competition in 1973 brought "The Villagers" the first ever major trophy in their 94-year history, and it was an emotional moment for player-coach Arthur Keegan *(left)* as he raised the trophy alongside winger Peter Goodchild. They had beaten Widnes on their own ground after defeating St.Helens in the semi-final.

FLOODLIT TROPHY FINALS IN THE 'SEVENTIES

1970-71
Tuesday 15th December 1970, at Headingley, Leeds.
Leeds 9, St.Helens 5.
Leeds: Try: Hynes. Goals: Holmes (2), Hynes.
St.Helens: Try: Jones. Goal: Coslett.
LEEDS: J.Holmes; A.Smith, S.Hynes, R.Cowan, J.Atkinson; A.Wainwright, M.Shoebottom; J.Burke, A.Fisher, T.Barnard, W.Ramsey, R.Haigh, R.Batten.
ST.HELENS: F.Barrow; L.Jones, W.Benyon, J.Walsh, F.Wilson; A.Whittle, J.Heaton; G.Rees, A.Karalius, E.Chisnall, J.Mantle, E.Prescott, K.Coslett.
Referee: Mr. E. Lawrinson (Warrington).
Attendance: 7,612. Receipts: £2,189.

1971-72
Tuesday 14th December 1971, at Knowsley Road.
St.Helens 8, Rochdale Hornets 2.
St.Helens: Goals: Coslett (4).
Rochdale: Goal: Chamberlain.
ST.HELENS: G.Pimblett; L.Jones, W.Benyon, J.Walsh, F.Wilson; K.Kelly, J.Heaton; G.Rees, A.Karalius, E.Chisnall, E.Prescott, J.Mantle, K.Coslett.
ROCHDALE HORNETS: J.Chamberlain; N.Brelsford, J.Crellin, D.Taylor, B.Glover; F.Myler, P.Gartland; P.Birchall, P.Clarke, E.Brown, R.Welding, W.Sheffield, H.Delooze. *Sub.:* A.Hodkinson (for Sheffield).
Referee: Mr. E. Clay (Rothwell).
Attendance: 9,255. Receipts: £2,208.

(Above) **Rochdale full-back in the 1971 Final, Joe Chamberlain**

1972-73
Tuesday 19th December 1972, at Central Park, Wigan.
Leigh 5, Widnes 0.
Leigh: Try: Lawson. Goal: Fiddler.
LEIGH: M.Hogan; G.Lawson, J.Atkins, M.Collins, M.Stacey; A.Barrow, C.Sayer; P.Grimes, D.Clarke, G.Fletcher, J.Fiddler, F.Barrow, T.Martyn.
Subs.: R.Lester (for Lawson), A.Ryding (for Sayer).
WIDNES: R.Dutton; A.Prescott, M.Aspey, R.Blackwood, P.McDonnell; G.Lowe, A.Ashton; J.Mills, K.Elwell, J.Warlow, J.Foran, B.Sheridan, G.Nicholls.
Referee: Mr. G. F. Lindop (Wakefield).
Attendance: 4,841. Receipts: £1,391.

1973-74
Tuesday 18 December 1973, at Naughton Park, Widnes.
Bramley 15, Widnes 7.
Bramley: Tries: Goodchild, Austin, Sampson.
Goals: Wolford (2), Ward.
Widnes: Try: Macko. Goals: Dutton (2).
BRAMLEY: A.Keegan; P.Goodchild, K.Bollon, J.Hughes, J.Austin; T.Briggs, B.Ward; D.Briggs, R.Firth, A.Cheshire, D.Sampson, G.Idle, J.Wolford.
Sub.: D.Ashman (for Ward).
WIDNES: R.Dutton; D.O'Neill, E.Hughes, M.Aspey, D.Macko; T.Warburton, R.Bowden; B.Hogan, K.Elwell, N.Nelson, B.Sheridan, R.Blackwood, D.Laughton.
Sub.: J.Foran (for Blackwood).
Referee: Mr. G. Kershaw (York).
Attendance: 4,542. Receipts: £1,538.

(Right)
The Leigh team celebrate in their dressing-room after winning the Floodlit Trophy in 1972, with a 5-nil victory over Widnes. The player holding the trophy in the middle of the group and already dressed in collar and tie and not rugby kit, is Leigh forward Paul Grimes who had been sent off in the match along with Widnes prop Jim Mills. This 1972 final was played at Wigan's Central Park, and was the only BBC Floodlit Trophy Final in the 'seventies to be staged on a neutral ground.

The prestige of winning the Floodlit Trophy resulted in several finals being intensely fought, low scoring affairs - as they had been in the competition's first four years in the 1960s. Lack of tries and high scores did not seem to dampen the enthusiasm of the television audiences, and one of the most exciting finals actually finished as a nil-nil draw, between Salford and Warrington in 1974. The Red Devils won the replay to put a rare piece of knockout cup silverware in the Willows' boardroom for a club which became synonymous with spectacular rugby under floodlights in the 'seventies.

1974-75

Tuesday 17th December 1974, at The Willows, Salford.
Salford 0, Warrington 0.
SALFORD: P.Charlton; K.Fielding, C.Hesketh, G.Graham, M.Richards; T.Brophy, P.Banner; M.Coulman, E.Devlin, A.Grice, J.Knighton, C.Dixon, E.Prescott. *Sub.: J.Taylor (for Brophy).*
WARRINGTON: D.Whitehead; D.Sutton, D.Cunliffe, A.Whittle, J.Bevan; W.Briggs, P.Gordon; D.Chisnall, K.Ashcroft, G.Wright, W.Gaskell, T.Conroy, B.Philbin. *Subs.: J.Lowe (for Cunliffe), P.Jewitt (for Philbin).*
Referee: Mr. W. H. Thompson (Huddersfield).
Attendance: 4,473. Receipts: £1,913.

Replay
Tuesday 28th January 1975, at Wilderspool, Warrington.
Salford 10, Warrington 0.
Salford: Tries: Fielding, Richards. Goals: Watkins (2).
SALFORD: F.Stead; K.Fielding, D.Watkins, C.Hesketh, M.Richards; K.Gill, P.Banner; A.Grice, P.Walker, G.Mackay, C.Dixon, J.Knighton, E.Prescott.
WARRINGTON: D.Cunliffe; D.Whitehead, W.Pickup, A.Whittle, J.Bevan; D.Noonan, P.Gordon; D.Chisnall, K.Ashcroft, R.Wanbon, T.Conroy, M.Nicholas, B.Philbin. *Subs.: W.Briggs (for Noonan), B.Brady (for Nicholas).*
Referee: Mr. W. H. Thompson (Huddersfield)
Attendance: 5,778. Receipts: £2,434.

1975-76

Tuesday 16th December 1975, at Knowsley Road.
St.Helens 22, Dewsbury 2.
St.Helens: Tries: Mathias (2), Benyon, Hull, Wilson.
Goals: Pimblett (2), Coslett. Drop-goal: Heaton.
Dewsbury: Goal: Stephenson.
ST.HELENS: G.Pimblett; L.Jones, W.Benyon, D.Hull, R.Mathias; F.Wilson, J.Heaton; J.Mantle, A.Karalius, M.James, G.Nicholls, E.Chisnall, K.Coslett.
DEWSBURY: J.Langley; J.Hegarty, G.Chalkley, I.Simpson, G.Mitchell; N.Stephenson, A.Bates; H.Beverley, R.Price, S.Hankins, S.P.Halloran, G.Bell, J.Grayshon. *Subs.: S.Lee (for Stephenson), P.Artis (for Halloran).*
Referee: Mr. W. H. Thompson (Huddersfield).
Attendance: 3,858. Receipts: £1,747.

1976-77

Tuesday 14th December 1976, at Hilton Park, Leigh.
Castleford 12, Leigh 4.
Castleford: Tries: Walsh, Burton. Goals: Lloyd (3).
Leigh: Try: Walsh. Drop-goal: Ashcroft.
CASTLEFORD: G.Wraith; S.Fenton, J.Joyner, P.Johnson, Jamie Walsh; B.Burton, G.Stephens; P.Khan, R.Spurr, A.Dickinson, M.Reilly, G.Lloyd, S.Norton.
LEIGH: M.Hogan; A.Prescott, M.Stacey, J.Woods, Joe Walsh; J.Taylor, C.Sayer; D.Chisnall, K.Ashcroft, G.Fletcher, D.Macko, P.Grimes, D.Boyd.
Referee: Mr. J. Jackson (Pudsey).
Attendance: 5,402. Receipts: £2,792.

That mould of low scoring was broken by a spectacular final between Hull K.R. and St.Helens at Craven Park in 1977, with all-time greats Clive Sullivan and Roger Millward getting winners' tankards. By this time the sponsorship money from the BBC had risen by over 50 per cent from the early years of the decade, to a total of £30,000. Some 22 clubs were entering the floodlit competition (in its inital years there were only eight entrants) and each received a £500 grant for taking part, the remaining £19,000 being distributed in prize money with the winner taking £5,000 and the runner-up £3,000.

Playing on a Tuesday night a week before Christmas might not have been the best time for drawing a crowd, but when local rivalry was involved that didn't matter as a capacity crowd of 18,500 packed the Boulevard to see Hull beat rivals Hull.K.R. in the last Floodit Trophy final in 1979.

(Right) **Hull F.C. second-rower Keith Boxall confronted by Hull K.R. stand-off Allan Agar in the 1979 "derby" Floodlit Trophy Final at a sold out Boulevard ground.**

1977-78
Tuesday 13th December 1977, at Craven Park, Hull.
Hull K.R. 26, St.Helens 11.
Hull K.R.: Tries: *Dunn (2), Smith, Sullivan, Hartley, Casey.* ***Goals:*** *Hall (4).*
St.Helens: Tries: *Glynn (2), Cunningham.*
Goal: *Glynn.*
HULL K.R.: D.Hall; G.Dunn, M.Smith, B.Watson, C.Sullivan; S.Hartley, R.Millward; J.Millington, D.Watkinson, John Cunningham, P.Lowe, P.Rose, L.Casey. *Sub.:* M.Hughes (for Cunningham).
ST.HELENS: G.Pimblett; L.Jones, D.Noonan, Eddie Cunningham, P.Glynn; W.Francis, K.Gwilliam; D.Chisnall, G.Liptrot, M.James, M.Hope, A.Karalius, H.Pinner.
Subs.: W.Platt (for Pimblett), N.Courtney (for Jones).
Referee: *Mr. M. J. Naughton (Widnes).*
Attendance: *10,099.* ***Receipts:*** *£6,586.*

1978-79
Tuesday 12 December 1978, at Knowsley Road, St.Helens.
Widnes 13, St.Helens 7.
Widnes: Tries: *Wright (2), Burke.* ***Goals:*** *Burke (2).*
St.Helens: Try: *Dave Chsinall.* ***Goals:*** *Pimblett (2).*
WIDNES: D.Eckersley; S.Wright, E.Hughes, M.Aspey, P.Shaw; M.Burke, R.Bowden; B.Hogan, K.Elwell, J.Mills, M.Adams, A.Dearden, D.Laughton.
ST.HELENS: G.Pimblett; L.Jones, P.Glynn, E.Cunningham, R.Mathias; W.Francis, N.Holding; D.Chisnall, G.Liptrot, M.James, G.Nicholls, J.Knighton, H.Pinner. *Sub.:* E.Chsinall (for Knighton).
Referee: *Mr. J. McDonald (Wigan).*
Attendance: *10,250.* ***Receipts:*** *£7,016.*

1979-80
Tuesday 18th December 1979, at the Boulevard, Hull.
Hull 13, Hull K.R. 3.
Hull: Tries: *Evans, Dennison, Birdsall.*
Goals: *Dennison (2).*
Hull K.R.: Try: *Hubbard.*
HULL: P.Woods; G.Bray, G.Evans, P.Coupland, S.Dennison; J.Newlove, K.Hepworth; K.Tindall, R.Wileman, V.Farrar, K.Boxall, R.Stone, S.Norton. *Sub.:* C.Birdsall (for Boxall).
HULL K.R.: I.Robinson; S.Hubbard, M.Smith, B.Watson, C.Sullivan; D.Hall, A.Agar; R.Holdstock, G.Tyreman, B.Lockwood, P.Lowe, G.Clarkson, P.Hogan. *Subs.:* S.Hartley (for Clarkson), J.Millington (for Hogan).
Referee: *Mr. W. H. Thompson (Huddersfield).*
Attendance: *18,500.* ***Receipts:*** *£16,605.*

(Above) **Hull Kingston Rovers captain Roger Millward lifts the BBC Floodlit Trophy in 1977, alongside him are David Hall and Mike Smith.**

THE GAME IN FRANCE

(Right)
Francis de Nadai leading France in the 1972 World Cup match versus Great Britain at Grenoble as Colin Dixon gives chase. The Limoux prop de Nadai played in the 1970 World Cup and returned to captain France in the 1972 tournament.

(Above)
Rene Mauries, as the President of the French League was its dominant figure throughout the 1970s.

Rene Mauries of Albi became the President of the French Rugby League in 1971 and for the rest of the decade was a powerful and determined leader, faced with the double ambition of developing a strong France team and also stabilising relations with the Rugby Union under the infamous 'Protocol' which many League followers were unhappy with. Mr. Mauries took on the challenge of staging the World Cup in 1972 and was committed to the expansion of the game, with attempts to set up new professional clubs in Pau and Grenoble. The latter part of the decade saw France achieve much success at international level, winning the European Championship in 1977 and then defeating Australia in both Tests in 1978 - the victories against the Aussies coming under a new coaching regime headed by Louis Bonnery and Roger Garrigue who took over from Antoine Jiminez in 1978.

CHAMPIONSHIP FINALS

1970 - St.Gaudens 32, beat X111 Catalan 10.
(At Toulouse - Att. 11,300.)
1971 - St.Esteve 13, beat St.Gaudens 4.
(At Toulouse - Att. 8,179.)
1972 - Carcassonne 21, beat St.Gaudens 9.
(At Toulouse - Att. 11,566.)
1973 - Toulouse 18, beat Marseille 0.
(At Toulouse - Att. 13,827.)
1974 - St.Gaudens 21, beat Villeneuve 8.
(At Toulouse - Att. 5,696.)
1975 - Toulouse 10, beat St.Esteve 9.
(At Toulouse - Att. 5,015.)
1976 - Carcassonne 14, beat Lezignan 6.
(At Toulouse - Att. 14,000.)
1977 - Albi 19, beat Carcassonne 10.
(At Albi - Att. 18,325.)
1978 - Lezignan 3, beat X111 Catalan 0.
(At Toulouse - Att. 10,358.)
1979 - X111 Catalan 17, beat Carcassonne 2.
(At Toulouse - Att. 13,202.)

(Above)
Roger Garrigue, played for France versus Australia in 1973 and then coached them to victory in 1978.

LORD DERBY CUP FINALS

1970 - Lezignan 14, beat Villeneuve 8.
(At Perpignan - Att. 7,640.)
1971 - Marseille 17, beat Lezignan 2.
(At Perpignan - Att. 6,310.)
1972 - St.Esteve 12, beat Villenueve 5.
(At Perpignan - Att. 8,250.)
1973 - St.Gaudens 22, beat Carcassonne 8.
(At Carcassonne - Att. 10,300.)
1974 - Albi 21, beat Lezignan 11.
(At Perpignan - Att. 6,580.)
1975 - Pia 9, beat Marseille 4.
(At Perpignan - Att. 9,021.)
1976 - X111 Catalan 23, beat Toulouse 8.
(At Perpignan - Att.11,000.)
1977 - Carcassonne 21, beat X111 Catalan 16.
(At Narbonne - Att. 10,085.)
1978 - X111 Catalan 18, beat Lezignan 7.
(At Narbonne - Att. 15,939.)
1979 - Villeneuve 15, beat Carcassonne 5.
(At Albi - Att. 6,642.)

AND IN AUSTRALIA

(*Above*) **Three of the most influentual figures in Australian Rugby League's rise in the 'Seventies, coach Jack Gibson with star players Ron Coote and Arthur Beetson after Easts' stunning Grand Final win in 1975.** (*Above, right*) **The captain of the 1973 Kangaroos, Graeme Langlands, with the Ashes trophy.**

Australia's home defeat to Great Britain in 1970 prompted a new approach to the coaching and development of young players which was to pay rich dividends for the Aussies as the decade progressed. At the same time the Sydney competition went surging ahead with an explosion in television coverage and sponsorship support. The first signs that something significant was stirring came when the Australian Schoolboys team visited England in 1972 and played a stunning brand of football. The coach of that schoolboy touring team, Roy Masters, became one of a group of coaches with premierships clubs from an educational background, along with men like Ted Glossop and Paul Broughton. In addition, coaches like Terry Fearnley and Jack Gibson (both former prop forwards) pioneered an interest in gaining new knowledge from American Football about the preparation of teams and physical fitness with the introduction of the Nautilus weight-training system..

It was Jack Gibson who emerged as the "master coach" in Australia, and the Eastern Suburbs team he guided to back to back premierships in 1974 and '75, was widely regarded as the best footballing outfit the game had seen. Easts won 19 straight games on their way to the title in 1975, with a team including two of Australia's "greats," Ron Coote and Arthur Beetson – both of whom captained their country during the 'Seventies. Easts also became the first Sydney club to carry a sponsors' name when City Ford paid them $150,000 over three years to have their name printed on the front of the famous tricolour jerseys.

The five-team play-off system was introduced in 1973, the year when the young Cronulla club made their first Grand Final appearance, losing to Manly in one of the most brutal games ever seen.

(*Above*)
Bob McCarthy in action for South Sydney, whom he helped to their last Grand Final wins in the early 'Seventies. Bob was also a regular in the Australian team and vice-captain of the 1973 Kangaroos.

SYDNEY GRAND FINALS

1970 - South Sydney 23, beat Manly 12. (*Att. 53,241.*)
1971 - South Sydney 16, beat St.George 10. (*Att. 62,828.*)
1972 - Manly 19, beat Eastern Suburbs 14. (*Att. 54,357.*)
1973 - Manly 10, beat Cronulla 7. (*Att. 52,044.*)
1974 - Eastern Suburbs 19, beat Canterbury 4. (*Att. 57,214.*)
1975 - Eastern Suburbs 38, beat St.George 0. (*Att. 63,047.*)
1976 - Manly 13, beat Parramatta 10. (*Att. 57,343.*)
1977 - St.George and Parramatta drew 9-9. (*Att. 65,959.*)
Replay: **St.George 22, beat Parramatta 0.** (*Att. 48,828.*)
1978 - Manly and Cronulla drew 11-11. (*Att. 51,510.*)
Replay: **Manly 16, beat Cronulla 0.** (*Att. 33,552.*)
1979 - St.George 17, beat Canterbury 13. (*Att. 50,991.*)

BRISBANE PREMIERSHIP WINNERS

1970 - Valleys; 1971 - Valleys; 1972 - Easts; 1973 - Valleys; 1974 - Valleys; 1975 - Wests; 1976 - Wests; 1977 - Easts; 1978 - Easts; 1979 - Valleys.

THE AMATEUR GAME

Amateur Rugby League staged a massive, and almost certainly life-saving, revolution in the 'seventies which, by the end of the decade, saw the game achieving things it could hardly have dreamt of before. That revolution came on 4th March 1973, when a meeting was called in the modest surroundings of the Greenside Working Men's Club, Wakefield Road, Huddersfield, by a group of enthusiasts desperate to do something to stop the alarming decline in the junior game. Up to that time, the Rugby Football League had been responsible for running the amateur side of the sport, but such was its crumbling state it was obvious that some serious surgery was needed if the amateur game was not going to be allowed to wither away completely. At that meeting in 1973 the British Amateur Rugby League Association was formed, established itself with a bank balance of £25, and with pioneers Jack Clayton (chairman), Tom Keaveney (secretary) and Maurice Oldroyd (assistant secretary), set about taking over the organisation of the amateur game. Initially they were met with strong opposition from the RFL and not all the amateur district leagues agreed to join BARLA at first, thus causing considerable turmoil. In an eerie replaying of history, the new BARLA organisation had been born in a spirit of rebellion in Huddersfield, just as the Rugby League (Northern Union) code itself had been born there almost 80 years earlier.

Although opposition from the RFL continued, BARLA made rapid progress in giving new impetus to the amateur game, and one of their first targets was achieved with the introduction of a National Amateur Cup in 1974, the first winners being Leigh Miners Welfare. The rumble of progress turned into an avalanche following the appointment of the visionary Brian Snape as the RFL's Chairman - one of the first things he did on taking office was call a meeting with BARLA in June 1974, at which the RFL's official approval was given to them as the independent governing body of amateur Rugby League. This was quickly followed by recognition from the Sports Council – giving BARLA the full mandate, and full confidence, to get on with things.

In March 1975, the annual amateur internationals with France were organised under the BARLA banner for the first time, with the British open-age side winning 10-4 at Lyon, and the Youth team (under-18s) losing home and away to the French, 21-0 at Villenueve and 8-2 at Headingley. By 1976 BARLA were able to appoint their first full-time staff member with Maurice Oldroyd becoming National Administrator and the following year a major landmark was achieved when the first ever tour to the southern hemisphere for amateur players took place. The 1977 BARLA Under-18s visit to Australia and New Zealand was staged in the Queen's Jubilee Year with officials of the Shaw Cross Boys Club in Dewsbury, Douglas Hird and Alan Lancaster, acting as the tour managers. Throughout the 'seventies they had been pioneering exchange tours for youth teams with French clubs. The captain of this first amateur touring side in 1977 was Terry McGovern from Simms Cross, Widnes, and the vice-captain was Ian Rudd of Wath Brow Hornets. The same

(Above)
Souvenir of BARLA's tour to Papua New Guinea in 1978, with captain Bob Colgrave pictured on the cover.

(Above)
Maurice Oldroyd, one of the pioneers of BARLA, pictured in 1975.

year, 1977, the British Amateur open-age team broke new ground by playing their international with France at Bastia, on the island of Corsica.

Something even bigger followed for BARLA in 1978 when the first ever southern hemisphere tour for Amateur open-age players took place.

With Bob Colgrave of Ace Amateurs (Hull) the team captain, and club mate Dennis Oaten the vice-captain, the British Amateurs undertook a 38-day tour involving nine matches, which took them to Australia, New Zealand and, most significantly, Papua New Guinea. This meant BARLA became the first sporting governing body anywhere in the world to send a team on a major tour to Papua New Guinea. It was certainly an eye-opening experience for all the British squad, not least when their second fixture, at Lae in the Northern Zone of Papua New Guinea, had to be abandoned in the 74th minute when a section of the packed crowd invaded the pitch and attacked the British players. History was made when the Great Britain Amateurs met the Papua New Guinea national team (the Kumuls) for the first time in a full international on 21 May 1978, the British players performing remarkably in such alien conditions of intense heat and humidity to win 28-7 in front of a capacity crowd of 14,500 in the capital, Port Moresby.

The following year in 1979 BARLA were able to host the Papua New Guinea team when they came to Europe for the first time – after touring in France, the Kumuls travelled to England and played three matches against BARLA teams: the St.Helens league, Cumbria and a return international with the Great Britain amateurs, who repeated their win of the previous year by beating the tourists 28-12 at the Boulevard ground in Hull.

Whilst all these new international horizons were opening up for BARLA, the strength of the amateur game was always going to be among its clubs and domestic competitions, and since the mid 'seventies the new confidence among amateur players had seen playing standards increase dramatically – as was clearly seen when amateurs lined up against professionals in cup competitions. In 1977, Cawoods of Hull, became the first amateur side to defeat a professional club in a major competition since 1909 when they knocked Halifax out of the Players No.6 Trophy, and some wonderful efforts were seen in the Challenge Cup. In 1976 Leigh Miners Welfare went down by just 16-12 against the previous year's Wembley finalists Warrington on their own ground at Wilderspool; then in 1977 Pilkington Recs' drew an incredible crowd of 11,261 to the St.Helens ground Knowsley Road, to see them take on Wigan and go down narrowly 10-4. And Pilks' repeated that excitement the following year in the Challenge Cup when they played a star-studded Castleford team at Knowsley Road, drawing another 11,000 crowd and losing a thrilling game 23-22. These sort of results and performances, to say nothing of the crowds, along with the overseas tours and ever growing number of youth teams, would have been unthinkable in the dark days of amateur Rugby League before BARLA was formed in 1973.

(Above)
**The Great Britain Amateur team in Papua New Guinea in 1978 when they made history as BARLA's first open-age touring side down-under.
Left to right:
(Back row): Ray Oldfield, Brian Harrop, Ray Dennett, Rod Lewis, David Dykes, Alan Varty, David Nicholson, Bob Colgrave (captain), Dennis Oaten, Peter Glover, John Eastwood, Colin Porthouse, Frank Jones, Sam Morton (coach), Harold Swift.
(Middle row): Bernard Southern, David Robinson, John Roberts, Jimmy Power, Paul Dowling, Steve Critchenson, Joey Hull, Doug Cooper, Roger Blair, Ron Carter.
(Front row): John McCabe, Stewart Berwick, Ernie Lowe, John Brown, Geoff Catling, Jimmy Green and Peter Moore.**

THE FINAL WORD

(Above) **Some of the newspaper headlines which shaped the decade of the 'Seventies.**

So that was the 'Seventies, and I hope readers have enjoyed this glance back at a decade which was so action-packed for Rugby League that it has been impossible to include all the material we would have liked. But, in a nutshell, the 1970s was the decade when Rugby League: switched from four tackles to six tackles; reduced the value of a drop-goal to just one point; began to attract major sponsorship; created new knockout competitions; split the league into two divisions; welcomed a new leadership regime at the RFL; established an independent organisation to control the amateur game; introduced the 'man of steel' award; and, for the first time in the history of the International Board, welcomed a new full member nation in Papua New Guinea.

And, after staging four World Cups in seven years, Rugby League realised that was too much and, instead, it was better the international game returned to the old cycle of major tours. That decision was made in 1977 at the same time as an international transfer ban was re-introduced to stem the flow of top British stars to Australian clubs – a move which prompted the then Great Britain coach David Watkins to suggest a period of dominance for the British would follow, going so far as to say "The Aussies may never beat us again." Well, things didn't quite work out that way, and we're still waiting to get our hands back on the Ashes which were last won by Great Britain in 1970 and lost in 1973. But the revival of the British game's morale which took place in the second half of the decade, thanks to the new RFL regime headed by David Oxley and David Howes along with the impact made by BARLA and a new coaching scheme, was never better illustrated than the contrast between the Kangaroo tours of 1973 and 1978. By the time the latter came around, and Headingley's 30,000 places were sold out almost overnight for the deciding third Ashes Test (compared to only 10,000 in 1973), it really did feel great to be a Rugby League fan. Those were truly exciting times, but so much came crashing down in the opening 40 minutes of that third Test, when the penny dropped that something else was happening to the game in Australia and we were being left behind.

For internationalists, the late 'Seventies opened up new avenues with the arrival on the scene of big Mike Mayer and his exciting plans to take the game to America, followed by the arrival of Papua New Guinea for their first tour to Europe. The game in France always held a fascination, ever since my friend Joe Chamberlain – after a long career with Rochdale Hornets and a brief spell player-coaching Barrow – went to the Racing Club of Albi and inspired them to victory in the French Cup in 1974. And the joy of seeing France defeat Australia in both Tests in the winter of 1978 is something that present day fans will never be able to appreciate. But there were sad moments, too, in a decade which saw the tragic death of Leeds player Chris Sanderson in 1977, followed the next year by an injury to the talented young Workington player John Burke which left him paralysed.

As for the printed word, the 1970s opened sadly with the end of *'Rugby League Magazine'* due to the untimely death of its editor A.N.Gaulton, but the *'Rugby Leaguer'* newspaper remained a constant throughout the decade as several short-lived publications came and went after just a couple of issues and a new weekly, *'Pro Ball,'* lasted only half a season in 1973, despite being given official backing by the RFL. In sharp contrast, a little magazine called *'Open Rugby'* first appeared in 1976 and, unlike so many others, did manage to stay the course - throughout the rest of the decade and beyond. And, it's fair to say, if *'Open Rugby'* hadn't happened, you would not be holding this book now.

Harry Edgar (Editor - 'Rugby League Journal')